SACRAMENTO PUBLIC LIBRARY
828 "I" STREET
SACRAMENTO, CA 95814

8/2006

SACRAMENTO PUBLIC LIBRARY

D0381239

.LECTIO'
C LIBRAR'

The Homeowner's Guide to

ENERGY INDEPENDENCE

The Homeowner's Guide to
ENERGY INDEPENDENCE
ALTERNATIVE POWER SOURCES
FOR THE AVERAGE AMERICAN

CHRISTINE WOODSIDE

THE LYONS PRESS
Guilford, CT 06437
An imprint of The Globe Pequot Press

To buy books in quantity for corporate use
or incentives, call **(800) 962–0973, ext. 4551,**
or e-mail **premiums@GlobePequot.com.**

Copyright © 2006 by Christine Woodside

ALL RIGHTS RESERVED. No part of this book may be reproduced or transmitted
in any form by any means, electronic or mechanical, including photocopying
and recording, or by any information storage and retrieval system, except as may
be expressly permitted in writing from the publisher. Requests for permission
should be addressed to The Lyons Press, Attn: Rights and Permissions Department,
P.O. Box 480, Guilford, CT 06437.

The Lyons Press is an imprint of The Globe Pequot Press

10   9   8   7   6   5   4   3   2   1

Printed in the United States of America

Designed by Sheryl P. Kober

Library of Congress Cataloging-in-Publication Data

Woodside, Christine, 1959–
The homeowner's guide to energy independence : alternative power sources for the
average American / Christine Woodside.
    p. cm.
  ISBN 13 978-1-59228-817-5
  ISBN 10 1-59228-817-0
Dwellings—Energy conservation. 2. Electric power production. 3. Dwellings—
Electric equipment. 4. Ecological houses. I. Title.
TJ163.5.D86W674 2005
333.79—dc22

                                        2005028063

THANKS TO . . .

Lilly Golden, who conceived of and edited this book.

All of the scientists and researchers whose work I have cited here.

Darlene Mariani, who assisted in research on alternative cars and solar incentive programs.

Nat Eddy, for explaining how solar photovoltaic cells work.

Annie Eddy, for advice and research on energy efficiency.

Elizabeth Eddy, for support.

Priscilla Martel and Valerie Fales, for their advice.

Holly Rubino, for leading me to this project.

Jim Schembari of *The New York Times* and Tom Condon of *The Hartford Courant*, who have worked with me on articles that grew into the solar energy chapter.

CONTENTS

8 – Conservation: Not a New Idea   107

Conservation has not caught on as a philosophy, because the energy supply is so plentiful. A brief history. Ways in which conservation has become mainstream: housing insulation, cleaner gasoline, cars with better miles-per-gallon performance.

9 - Conservation Tips   119

A list of actions to cut back on energy consumption.

10 - An Appliance Manifesto   135

A call for every citizen to discard energy hogs.

Appendix: Where to Learn More.   145

General Information about Energy Consumption
and Alternatives

Notes   159

Index   171

INTRODUCTION

Oil prices have risen so fast since the late 1990s
that in a few years' time, alternative energy has lost its association
with latter-day hippies living in yurts. Electricity supplies were
stumbling during high-use summer periods ever since the late 1990s,
but the price of oil started to spike in late 2004, and that really got
the public's attention. Over a few-month period in late 2004, the
price of a barrel of oil shot up by 30% to more than $40 a barrel—
and soon after started breaking records as it approached $60. In one
year, from June 2004 to June 2005, average automobile fuel prices in
the United States rose by 9¢, and when the summer travel season
started, a gallon of gas was more than $2.10. Then, after Hurricane
Katrina, it spiked to over $3. Clearly, we live in volatile times,
energy-wise. The reality of enjoying cheap oil has started to lose its
grounding, even though oil is still relatively cheaper than most alternative forms of energy like the sun and the wind. Many factors, from
economic predictions to political tensions to war, influence oil
prices—but one factor is coming into ever-sharper focus: the world's
oil reserves are dipping ever lower, and someday in the next generation or two, it won't be the cheapest and most efficient way to power
the majority of society.

We have dealt with short-term problems, such as those experienced this decade when oil producers tried to cut their costs and a few unusually cold winters led people to burn more petroleum than usual.[1] More ominous are the long-term worries. Petroleum, natural gas, and coal are all finite resources. Political leaders have understood this for decades.

And yet, from the point of view of ordinary citizens like me and you, the country seems stalled at the point where we're worrying about whether to worry about it yet. Adjusted for inflation, car gas is still much cheaper than it was in the late 1970s.[2] Adjusted for inflation, crude oil still costs less than it did in 1980 (about $81 in today's money) or in 1864 (about $92 in today's money). But how desperate do we want to be before we look for other ways to power our lives, to keep warm, and to travel? Ordinary people are starting to ask why providing basic needs like heat and hot water must rely on a supply of oil that will run out in their children's lifetimes. Experts predict that in the next half century, petroleum reserves will reach a point too low to yield a benefit. As we approach that point, petroleum will continue to cost ever more as the supply dips low, which leads us to conflicts with the oil-rich Middle East. Listening to the evening news can leave the average American feeling helpless about our dependence on foreign countries, some of them hostile to us, for that most basic need: fuel.

It's not just that the supplies are low. Burning all fossil fuels has been linked with the quickening trend of global warming. Scientists almost universally agree that the rise in the average yearly temperature on Earth over the past century is the result of humans releasing large amounts of carbon dioxide into the atmosphere by burning oil, coal, and natural gas. Most of this continent's electricity generation, home heating, and transportation burn fossil fuels.

Have you ever felt like pulling away from this dependence on fossil fuels? I have, and yet I realized I didn't know the first thing about how to do it. I'm an average East Coast dweller burning up fossil fuel resources in my car and in my house. I live with my husband and our two teenaged daughters in an 1,100-square-foot Victorian house in a tiny Connecticut town. My family considers itself frugal and environmentally conscious. We keep the thermostat low, turn it down at night, and turn off the lights when we go to sleep. We aren't big television watchers. We have one home computer and no microwave. We cook from scratch on a propane stove and use a water-saving shower nozzle. So I felt irritated and powerless when utility deregulation and supply shortages started to affect my region of the country a few years ago. I started to pay attention to our electric bills.

One of our recent bills for one month, between mid-January and mid-February 2005, came to $216.37 for 1,694 kilowatt-hours of power. (Including all of the transmission and distribution surcharges in my state, the rate came to almost 13¢ per kilowatt-hour. Since then it has risen to 14.5¢ per kilowatt-hour.) In southern New England, oil-burning plants still provide much of the electricity. But this story of rising power demand and uncertain energy supplies is playing out in varying ways across the country. My family's skyrocketing bills—roughly twice what we paid only five years ago—forced me to consider electricity and where it comes from. I quickly learned that we are paying not only much more than we budgeted for electricity, but that we are using almost twice as much electricity as the average household in our state, even though we have a small house and don't heat with electricity. (We heat with an oil-burning furnace.) It's still a puzzle to us, but it appears that our electric hot water heater is the main culprit.

The same month, I talked to Ed Witkin, who lives west of me in Bridgewater, Connecticut, with his wife, Ellen Shrader, and two daughters. Their modern house runs almost entirely on solar energy. They are not connected to the electric grid; no wires extend up their long driveway from the street to their house. Forced by their own choice to be careful with power, they have settled into a routine of using no more than 150 kilowatt-hours a month. The Witkin-Shrader family is the same size as ours—two adults and two teenaged daughters—and the house itself is larger than ours. They manage to use one-tenth of what we use in the winter (which is our highest-use time because we don't have air-conditioning). They don't sit in the dark, wash in frigid water, or cook on an open fire. Like my family, they own one computer and do without a microwave. Their daughters take long, hot showers just as ours do, they have a propane kitchen stove similar to ours, and they, too, watch a little television. But here, they depart from us. Their refrigerator (a Sun Frost) is an ultra-low-energy brand while ours is not. They heat water with solar collectors on their roof, while we heat our water with electricity. They use compact fluorescent bulbs in all of their fixtures, while we have replaced only two so far in our house. My family is using ten times the energy they are.

Why is that? We, like most Americans, are hooked into a way of life that uses too much energy. We might not be wasteful people by nature, but we go about our business without the feeling that we should turn things off. It does not seem to be an emergency to replace our ten-year-old refrigerator. Someday we'll get around to replacing the bulbs. We sometimes leave on lights and appliances when we're not using them. The Witkin-Shraders are not like this. They pay attention to everything that is running—because they are collecting their own energy at their house, and they don't want to run out. We, on the other hand, know that more energy will always be there for us, as long as we pay for it.

It's been difficult facing up to this. My husband and I didn't think we were such energy hogs. We try to conserve energy and resources by limiting the appliances we use, driving used cars, and living in a small house. We use a vintage 1993 refrigerator. Now we must face the reality that this machine, even though it isn't worn out, burns four times the energy the most advanced new model does. Our top-loading washing machine is older, but because it still operates, we don't want to throw it out. The machine uses more power and water than the new front-loading tumble washers. We rely on what we thought was an efficient electric water heater, bought only a few years ago. But now we are starting to believe that heating water with electricity is wasteful.

Until recently, when I compared my house to Ed Witkin's, I did not realize that a family like mine could help our greater world stop depending on fossil fuels. I have realized that our 1,100-square-foot Victorian house can drastically cut its energy consumption. The four of us who live in this house can also make choices that turn some of the decisions about energy over to the grassroots of America. In our way, we can begin to change the world by refusing to depend solely on distant sources of fossil fuels. It makes sense morally, financially, and, most of all, environmentally.

How do we do it? Making the move to using less energy isn't an easy choice in financial terms, for us and for most middle-class people. New appliances cost hundreds or thousands of dollars. If we buy a new refrigerator and a low-energy washing machine, we know we will eventually recoup the money in saved energy. But we can't put up money for both of these at the same time. It's not good to go bankrupt—so we have to figure out how to change things step by step. And we want to take action individually: We don't want to sit home and hope the large utilities will start using the sun or the wind and thus make changes for us.

How quickly can consumers recoup investments in alternative energy sources? More and more of the new technologies aren't out of the realm of affordability. We will probably have to borrow money or liquidate savings to install a solar photovoltaic system, which today in my state of Connecticut requires at least $15,000 to $20,000 after the state rebate. In all likelihood we will wait at least fifteen years to recoup the money in saved energy. That's not too bad considering that the panels usually last twenty-five years. Efficient appliances can pay for themselves in a few years. Gas-electric hybrid cars can pay for themselves in even less time, depending on the model you choose. Yes, we will get that money back, and yes, we will begin to get away from the old ways as soon as we make these choices. In almost all cases, you eventually recoup your investment of money. Environmentally, you and the rest of the planet begin to receive benefits the second you make the switch.

To make the leap to alternative energy means you are ahead of your time—but only slightly. Fossil fuels, and especially oil, dominate the energy supplies in North America today, but interest in alternative energy is on the rise. It is getting easier to find information and to buy products that use other sources, such as the sun or wind. After the last major flush of interest in alternative energy, during the oil crisis of the 1970s, alternative energy retreated into a subculture, bringing to mind back-to-the-land hippies in sandals, building shacks in the northern territories. That isn't true anymore.

It can't remain true, even if we could pay for all this oil we think we need. Oil will not retain its power past the next generation of Americans. Experts report that the world is at its peak oil use right about now and that oil supplies will dip dramatically by 2050. Oil will take a fall unless a huge unfound reserve shows up sometime in the next decade or so. (See chapter 1 for more about this.)

Don't wait for alternative energy to become mainstream. Take steps as an individual now and create the demand for alternative energy that assures it *will* become mainstream. Whether you live in the city, the suburbs, or the country, you can take steps toward independence immediately. Most important: we use more power than we have to right now. We must stop looking at alternative energy as a direct substitute for oil. Yes, we can use alternative energy sources instead of oil, but we also have to commit to using less energy overall.

You can save money in the long term by spending money in the short term. Begin by experimenting with the two most viable and affordable alternative energy sources: solar panels and wind generators.

Solar: The typical 4-kilowatt solar photovoltaic system pays for itself in roughly fifteen years in many states, thanks to state government rebates. Note that these rebates are funded by electric bill surcharges; you're already paying for the rebates. Rebates are now available in twenty-three states. In solar hot-water systems, pipes filled with antifreeze solutions absorb the sun's heat and circulate through pipes submerged in water tanks, providing half to all of a household's hot water. (See chapter 2.)

Wind: Until you have watched a wind generator with long, slim blades made blurry from the constant turning, you haven't fully appreciated the possibilities of clean energy. Today you can buy wind generators for your own yard, if they're tall enough to catch at least nine miles per hour of wind. (See chapter 3.)

Next, inform yourself of the still-experimental technologies.

Hydrogen fuel cells: While you can't buy a hydrogen fuel cell for your basement yet, governments and private industries here and abroad are experimenting with tiny to large units, in which a chemical reaction splits the hydrogen atom, allowing its electrons to make power in a circuit before rejoining the protons. Oxygen gets released as water vapor. The talk is that someday hydrogen fuel cells will power everything from cell phones to heating and cooling systems, creating a power revolution we haven't seen in a century. Iceland announced in 1999 that it would become the world's first hydrogen economy. Major corporations such as Shell Hydrogen and Daimler-Chrysler are working on the technology. (See chapter 4.)

Vegetable oil fuel: The original diesel engine was designed for use with vegetable oil. Biodiesel fuel is a mixture of regular diesel and vegetable oil–based fuel or pure vegetable oil–based fuel, designed for diesel engines. (See chapter 4.)

Geothermal heat pumps: Dig down far enough and you find heat. Geothermal heat pumps are set up to funnel this heat into a house during the winter and to use the heat as energy to blow out hot air in the summer, thereby acting as both a cooling and heating system. (See chapter 4.)

Wood: It's within your power to burn wood cleanly in a newer stove that's properly cleaned and maintained. Wood supplies are plentiful enough, the technology is there to filter out particulate pollution, and as long as you have an inexpensive source of wood, you can save hundreds to more than a thousand dollars each year. (See chapter 5.)

Hydroelectric: The power of a stream or small river can provide a lot of electricity to your home, but the cost is so high that your reasons must go beyond economics. Learn about the fascinating ways to harness water in chapter 6.

Alternative cars: Gas-electric hybrid cars recharge an electric battery as they go, switching back and forth from gas power to electric power. Hundreds of thousands of these cars are now on sale in this country. New models are coming out—even hybrid sport utility vehicles. Their prices are similar to traditional cars, so you can recoup your investment very quickly. (See chapter 7.)

Use less energy—the quickest and best thing to do: While conservation has yet to catch on as a habit in the United States, we must learn to conserve. It's the most basic and important act we can perform. I have realized that the best way to conserve energy is to force ourselves into crisis mode. We must learn to think of conservation as our response to a crisis that much of our world hasn't yet accepted. It's not hard to conserve, but it means we have to go against the grain of our friends and family and start thinking differently. High on my list for my family will be to replace our old refrigerator with one that uses half of the energy. We can buy this as soon as we have the funds for it. Then I'm going to replace the washer. But I'm also going to start hanging most of the laundry on a clothesline, use compact fluorescent bulbs in most of the fixtures, and limit my uses of hot water by taking shorter showers and by not leaving water running while I rinse dishes. (See chapters 8 and 9 for more ideas on conserving energy.)

Beyond any financial gain we achieve in a campaign to use alternative energy at the grassroots level is the more important gain of using clean energy to ensure a healthier planet Earth. Two generations from now, these methods and fuels must replace fossil fuels. We can start to do this before the stock market puts the change in place by tracking the growing worry in the marketplace. I don't mean to sound cynical, but when it comes to the economy, who knows when that will happen? We little people can gently force the issue—and we can do this now.

The Homeowner's Guide to
ENERGY
INDEPENDENCE

CHAPTER ONE

The Situation Today: Oil Rules

America depends on fossil fuels, particularly oil, to support life as we know it. Fossil fuels provide about 85% of the world's energy sources. Petroleum is the largest pool, providing about 40%. Nearly tied for second place are natural gas (about 23%) and coal (about 22%). It remains relatively cheap to find and use fossil fuels.[1] These fossil fuels provide the vast majority of energy for electricity, heat, and transportation in houses, apartments, and industry. But they can't do this indefinitely. Experts have predicted that petroleum reserves will peter out in around 2050.[2]

Such predictions have been widely touted for decades, but as a nation, Americans don't seem worried—judging by our consumption of fossil fuels. We have not made the connection between our own habits, actions, and needs and the diminishing fuel reserves that fulfill them. We have lived with incredible plenty for half a century. But the government, which continues to promote oil drilling, also tells citizens to conserve energy. Leaders do this because they can't ignore the disconnect between Americans' consumption and our reliance on foreign oil. In 2005, the U.S. Congress passed energy legislation that will encourage more oil and gas production in the United States. The bill, signed into law in August 2005, provides $14.5 billion in tax incentives, most of it going to oil and gas companies. Here is what President George W. Bush said in a speech in June 2005: "Our dependence on foreign oil is like a foreign tax on the American Dream—and that tax is growing every year." For the short term, though, the U.S. government is wedded to oil. "We're encouraging oil-producing countries to maximize their production, so more crude oil is on the market to meet the demands of the world," he said.[3]

You can get upset about this or be patient about America's predicament, but you can't deny the ordinary American's part in this situation. We rely on fossil fuels to feed not only industry and transportation, but our own habits—our own way of life.

The federal government has supported funds to develop alternative cars, hydrogen fuel cells, and to boost energy conservation. Energy proposals introduced under Bush also included research into mixing ethanol—produced by growing corn in the Midwest—with regular gasoline, and studying hydrogen fuel cells. Leaders are more focused, though, on finding new sources of oil, building nuclear power plants, and mining and burning more coal.

Consider also the clear links scientists have established between fossil-fuel burning and the global-warming trend of the last fifty years. The fundamentally damaging aspect of fossil fuels is that when they burn, they release carbon that was stored in the ground millions of years ago. Fossil fuels form in the earth over a period of millions of years through slow decomposition and change. It does not appear that people can speed up that process to make more petroleum, coal, or natural gas. Today when scientists and policy makers argue about fossil fuels and global warming, they seem to argue most about how much we should worry about the dwindling supplies. No one will try to argue that fossil fuels won't eventually run out. They will.

How soon will they run out?

COAL

Scientists predict that at the current rate of consumption, coal supplies will probably last a long time—from between 250 and 350 years.[4] That sounds promising, but we have yet to find a method of burning coal cleanly.

Coal is fossilized peat, or very old remains of plants that were originally wet in a bog or marsh. It burns easily and is plentiful in North America. The United States holds a quarter of the world's coal reserves. Coal comes in different forms: about half of it is bituminous and anthracite coal. The other half is subbituminous and lignite coal. But the air pollution caused by burning coal, especially particulate pollution, has continued to cause health and visibility problems. Technology hasn't been able to completely clean up coal, which is too bad, because the supply is plentiful. The pollution from coal-fired power plants in the Midwest and car and truck traffic has created haze over a good part of the East Coast.

OIL

The major fuel source in America is oil, by which I mean petroleum.[5] The world's oil supplies will effectively run out—meaning that our ability to extract oil will be so diminished that it won't be worth doing so—by about 2050. Oil is old stuff. It formed over a period of millions of years, when the remains of plants and animal carcasses washed into the oceans and, with sand, piled up in layers. Pressure changed the sand to rock, while the organic material changed into petroleum. Oil combines hydrogen and carbon molecules. It travels or seeps up from the rock crevices where it formed, through tiny holes in the rock, or it remains trapped in underground oil reservoirs.[6]

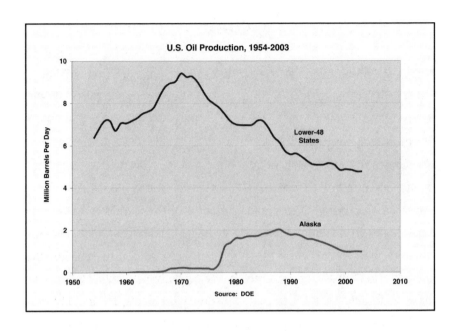

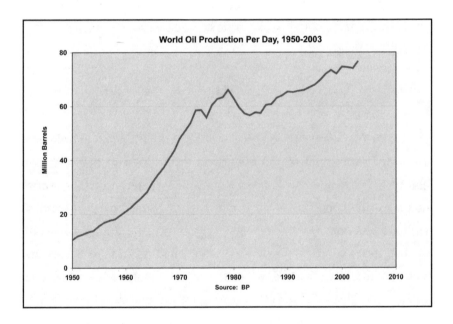

SOURCE: Charts courtesy of the Worldwatch Institute

The demand for oil continues to rise while the world's oil producers have begun to struggle to keep up with the demand. The World-watch Institute, an independent environmental research group in Washington, D.C., reported in 2005 that the stable oil prices of the 1990s will probably not return in the near future. Oil production might not be able to meet the expected demand as early as the middle of the next decade.[7]

While America continues to need oil to run most of its infrastructure, other countries wait in line for it, too. Japan is the second-largest importer of oil in the world. China's development explosion has increased that giant country's demand for oil. The story is similar in other countries that are growing, Western-style, and whose leaders want the same quality of life Americans now expect. Still, Americans use more oil, person for person, than any other nationality. We use a quarter of the world's oil and produce about 8% of it (even though our land contains only 2% to 3% of that supply).

Scientists began predicting the oil supply's peak and decline in the 1940s. M. King Hubbert, a geologist for Shell Oil Company, used his field knowledge to predict that American oil production would peak in 1970 and drop after then. That has come true. The Hubbert's Peak (or Peak Oil) referred to a bell curve he plotted estimating the height of production capability (based upon supply)—after which less oil would be found year after year, until the supply ran out. The United States hit its own 'peak oil' production in the 1970s and has been producing less oil since that time, making up the difference with imports. The Alaskan pipeline slowed the drop in American production but did not reverse it; three-fourths of the oil in Prudhoe Bay has been pumped. The Arctic National Wildlife Refuge, a potential pumping ground long fought over in the U.S. Congress, probably contains much less oil than Alaska did. Oil production in the Gulf of Mexico has been declining since 1970.

Looking elsewhere in the world, peak oil was originally predicted to hit in 1995, but this did not take into account the Arab oil embargo of the 1970s. The latest guess is that the peak has happened, or sometime very soon it will hit in places like the Middle East. (See highlights of U.S. Representative Roscoe G. Bartlett's speech on page 17.)[8]

Oil certainly will not remain abundant and cheap past the next generation, and even if it hangs on a few decades after that, the trend toward scarcity won't reverse.

A potentially giant source of oil lies buried in North American shale. The region includes a large area in Colorado. The cost of extracting that oil, however, could be so high that the potential of this source is thrown into doubt. And that, too, would not last forever.[9]

America established a stockpile of emergency oil in 1975. The first deliveries began in 1977. The oil is stored in salt caverns on the Gulf of Mexico coast in Texas and Louisiana. The Strategic Petroleum Reserve (SPR) held about 670 million barrels as of late 2004. This is the largest emergency supply in the world. The Department of Energy explains that the country would dip into this supply during a "severe energy supply interruption" that they define as "of significant scope and duration" or a problem that "may cause major adverse impact on national safety or the national economy (including an oil price spike)" or an emergency due to "an interruption in the supply of imported petroleum products, or from sabotage or an act of God." The supply was tapped to ease shortages after Hurricane Katrina damaged refineries and portals on the Louisiana coast in 2005.[10]

Unsettling.

The arguments in favor of oil remain largely economic. It's cheap. Many political leaders focus on oil because, so far, there is still enough and it still costs less to extract what's left than to invest time and money in bringing alternative energy sources into the mainstream

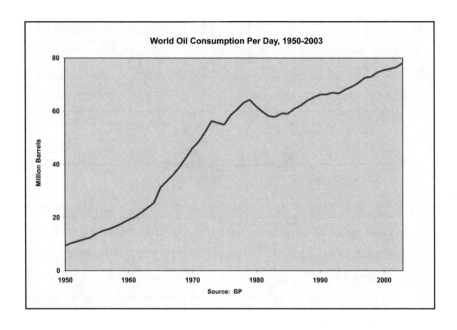

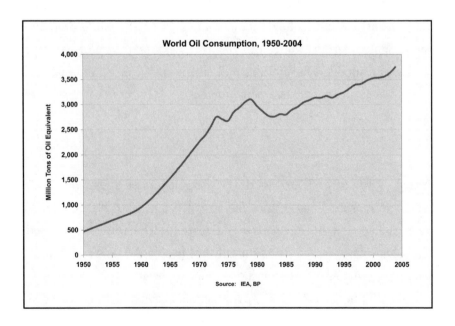

SOURCE: Charts courtesy of the Worldwatch Institute

and to create an infrastructure to support them. The U.S. government is studying alternative energy, but we remain far from an infrastructure that relies on it. We still look for oil. Meanwhile, the air quality is not improving, even with better ways of filtering smokestacks and car mufflers.

NATURAL GAS

Natural gas is a mixture of carbon (about 75%), hydrogen, nitrogen, and a small amount of oxygen. Natural gas is transported in giant tankers in liquefied form. It arrives in houses via a system of about 250,000 miles of buried pipes. Natural gas supplies are expected to last until between 2050 and about 2085.[11] We still rely on other countries for most of our supply. It's found in many places around the world, with most of it in the Middle East (more than 24%) and Russia (23%). North America holds more than 17% of the world's supply. Since September 11, 2001, the security risks of transporting huge tankers of liquefied natural gas and storing it in giant terminals on coastlines has emerged as a new problem.

It always comes back to the truths about all fossil fuels. We aren't making any more. They pollute the air when burned, dirty the oceans when spilled, and, in the case of coal, create health hazards and scarred landscapes when mined. In the meantime, people in many countries—particularly Americans—are using ever more power.

Starting in the late 1990s, power supplies couldn't meet the summer peak demands in California. Brownouts (reductions in the flow of electricity, making lights dim or flicker) became common and the threat of blackouts (total power outages) turned people's eyes toward the power grid in the summer, the season of highest electricity usage. It's common to call the electric distribution system *the grid*, or the *power grid*. What is this thing that has become part of our folk history? The power grid is the system of interconnected high-voltage lines in the United States (and parts of Canada), which carry power from power plants to where the power is needed. The term often includes the local distribution networks. There are more than 6,000 power plants in the United States. The power from these plants travels on a half-million miles of high-voltage transmission lines. Their transmission to localized areas is handled through 100 control centers where workers and automatic switching can direct the power to areas where it's most needed. Electricity funnels to local areas through substations, which "step down" the power to lower current. You have probably seen these jumbles of wires behind fences near your home.

Because the grid is interconnected, a lightning strike or a particularly high power demand from one region of the country can cut the power flow to other regions. Some of the major blackouts in history were started by one localized problem. The Northeast blackout of 1965 started when one line tripped in Ontario.[12] The August 14, 2003, blackout that left 50 million people without electricity in eight states and Ontario began with high demand and outages in Cleveland and Akron.[13]

Reading the papers, listening to the radio, surfing the Web, checking out some of the new books coming out, and watching television, I can't seem to get away from this problem of diminishing fossil fuel. That's good. A few years ago, no one talked much about it. Now the rising prices have the topic coming up every week. Americans are starting to understand, to really get it: unless a huge unfound reserve that's easily pumped shows up sometime in the next decade or so, people must figure out another way of producing electricity and heat. The alternative energy sources won't allow us to simply plug our energy-gobbling ways of life into new technology. We're going to have to learn to use less electricity and fuel than we have been enjoying for most of my forty-six years, during which time, the world population has doubled. The experts are telling us that life will have to change. Author James Kunstler, a brilliant critic of our wasteful oil-gobbling habits, calls the future "the Long Emergency."[14] The scientists James A. Frey and Dan S. Golumb say, "For the sake of husbanding the fossil fuel reserves, as well as for the sake of mitigating air pollution and the CO_2-caused global warming, mankind ought to conserve these fuels, increase the efficiency of their uses, and shift to non-fossil energy sources."[15]

FEDERAL ENERGY POLICY ACT HIGHLIGHTS

In 2005, the federal government passed an energy law that funnelled billions of dollars in subsidies to traditional energy sources such as fossil fuels and large hydroelectric projects, leading to criticism by many groups.

The bill was not only about fossil fuel. It did fund some studies and incentives for alternative energy. Here are some of the provisions:

- Major improvements to the nation's electricity capacity and transmission.

- More domestic oil and gas exploration, and increased access to federal lands for this purpose. While Congress has never approved proposals to drill in the Arctic National Wildlife Refuge (ANWR), drilling in this region could resurface as a new proposal at any time.

- $2.8 billion for fossil fuel production.

- Expanding the Strategic Petroleum Reserve from 700 million to 1 billion barrels, adding the oil during non-emergency times.

- An accelerated approval process for new oil refineries in targeted areas.

- $4.3 billion for the development of more nuclear power plants.

- $1.8 billion for the Clean Coal Power Initiative, which will support coal-burning power plants that reduce air pollution, mostly through coal gasification, a method of burning coal that converts it into a gas which then can make electric power.

- Loan guarantees for gasification of a petroleum by-product, petroleum coke, for an energy source.

- Programs to promote coal as a fuel and to clean emissions in coal-fired power plants.

- $100 million for increased production at hydroelectric power plants.

- An increase in the amount of ethanol and other biofuel additives in gasoline.

- $2.1 billion over five years for research into hydrogen vehicles, with a goal to get them on the road by 2020.

- $200 million in grants to states and cities to buy alternative-fuel buses.

- Tax credits for buying gas-electric hybrid vehicles.

- Incentives for renewable energy including solar, wind, hydro-electric, biomass, and landfill gas.

- A 20% reduction in energy use in federal buildings by 2015 and money for energy efficiency programs in public buildings.

- A goal for the federal government to use at least 7.5% renewable energy by 2013.

- More than $10 billion over three years for the federal Low Income Housing Assistance Program. More money for the poor to weatherize their homes.

- Expansion of the federal Energy Star program that promotes energy-efficient appliances.

- Rebates for renewable energy systems for houses and small businesses.

- A longer period of Daylight Saving Time. Clocks will move ahead one hour on the second Sunday in March instead of the first Sunday of April. The return to standard time will be the first Sunday in November instead of the last Sunday of October.

- A ban of the gasoline additive MTBE, which was found to contaminate groundwater.

SOURCE: U.S. House Committee on Energy and Commerce,
http://energycommerce.house.gov.

So much of the energy matters the country faces still swirl around oil. We are not yet turning the entire country toward alternatives. It's natural to wonder why the country remains in the research stages when oil is running out and the environmental damage it's doing seems to worsen each year. Instead of trying to answer that difficult question, an ordinary citizen can ask a more practical question, to which there is an answer: What can I do?

The thing for a little person to do when he looks at the big picture and doesn't see enough change unfolding is to take action on the small level. Start at your house or apartment, and begin, step by step, to move away from fossil fuels. It's not practical to do this all at once, unless you are a millionaire. But within a several-year period, you can take steps that transform your house into a place that produces and conserves energy, rather than one that simply uses it and pays for it. Maybe you can't cut out all fossil-fuel use, but you can greatly diminish the amount you buy—and therefore contribute to cleaner air now and a better future. Instead of hoping that the world's political leaders will institute big policy changes that make these distant power plants operate off the sun, the wind, or some technology yet to be perfected, institute your own personal policy changes at home. Make your own energy. Sell your power back to your leaders if you can—or if you want to. Take steps toward independence. It's the American way. The antidote to discouragement is action.

Americans and Energy

Net Electricity Generation (2004): 3,921 billion kilowatt-hours.

Electricity End Use Consumption (2004): 3,735 billion kilowatt-hours.

Total Energy Consumption (2003): 98.1 quadrillion British thermal units (BTUs), equaling 25% of world total energy consumption. (Total energy consumption includes petroleum, dry natural gas, coal, net hydroelectric, nuclear, geothermal, solar, wind, wood, and waste electric power.)

Renewable Energy Consumption (2003): 6.1 quadrillion BTUs, about 45% of which was conventional hydroelectric power. (Renewable energy data from the International Energy Agency includes hydropower, solar, wind, tide, geothermal, solid biomass and animal products, biomass gas and liquids, industrial and municipal wastes.)

Energy-Related Carbon Dioxide Emissions (2002): 5,796 million metric tons of carbon (about 24% of world total carbon emissions).

Per Capita Energy Consumption (2003): 338 million BTUs.

Per Capita Carbon Dioxide Emissions (2002): 20.3 metric tons.

Residential Energy Use, Expressed as Percentage of the Whole: 22%.

Transportation Energy Use, Expressed as a Percentage of the Whole: 27%.

Fuel Share of Energy Consumption (2003): Oil (40%), Coal (23%), Natural Gas (23%), Nuclear (8%), Hydroelectricity (3%), Other "Renewables" (3%).

Fuel Share of Carbon Dioxide Emissions: Oil (44%), Coal (36%), Natural Gas (20%).

Oil Consumption (as of October 2004): 20.4 million barrels per day.

U.S. Oil Production: 7.7 million barrels per day, of which 5.4 million is crude oil (as of 2004).

Proven Oil Reserves (as of January 2005, according to *Oil & Gas Journal*): 21.9 billion barrels.

Net Oil Imports (as of October 2004): 11.8 million barrels per day, or 58% of total consumption.

Gross Oil Imports (as of 2003): 12.2 million barrels per day, of which, 9.6 million was crude oil and 2.6 million were petroleum products.

Crude Oil Imports from the Persian Gulf (as of October 2004): 2.4 million barrels per day.

Top Sources of U.S. Crude Oil Imports (as of October 2004): Canada (1.61 million barrels per day); Mexico (1.59 million barrels per day); Saudi Arabia (1.48 million barrels per day); Venezuela (1.29 million barrels per day); Nigeria (1.09 million barrels per day).

Total Oil Stocks (as of December 2004): 1.65 billion barrels (including about 673 million barrels in the U.S. Strategic Petroleum Reserve).

Natural Gas Reserves (as of January 2005, according to *Oil & Gas Journal*): 189 trillion cubic feet.

Dry Natural Gas Production (as of 2004): 18.7 trillion cubic feet.

Natural Gas Consumption (as of 2004): 21.9 trillion cubic feet.

Gross Natural Gas Imports (2004): 4.1 trillion cubic feet (about 87% from Canada).

Coal Consumption (2004): 1,102 million short tons.

Coal Production (2004): 1,105 million short tons.

Gross Coal Exports (2004): 51 million short tons.

Gross Coal Imports (2004): 27 million short tons.

Primary and Secondary Coal Stocks (August 2004): 150 million short tons.

Electric Net Summer Installed Capacity (2002): 905 giga-watts (76% thermal-fired, 11% nuclear; 11% hydroelectric, and 2% "renewables").

Oil Pipelines: Around 2 million miles.

Natural Gas Transmission Pipelines: 250,000 miles.

SOURCE: U.S. Department of Energy, Energy Information Administration, which cites the following sources:

The Associated Press; *Christian Science Monitor; Dallas Morning News;* Dow Jones; *EIU Viewswire; Energy Daily; Energy Report; Financial Times; Financial Times Energy Newsletters; Gas Daily; Global Insight; Houston Chronicle; Los Angeles Times; Megawatt Daily; The New York Times; Oil & Gas Journal; Oil Daily; Petroleum Intelligence Weekly; Pipeline and Gas Journal; Platts Oilgram News; PR Newswire;* Reuters; U.S. Energy Information Administration (numerous publications—see links); *USA Today; Washington Post; Weekly Petroleum Argus; World Gas Intelligence; World Markets Online; World Oil.*

For definitions of measurements:
http://www.eia.doe.gov/glossary/glossary_m.htm

"We pay more for water in the grocery store
than we pay for gas at the pump . . ."
—*Roscoe G. Bartlett*

Excerpts of a sparsely attended speech on the "Peak Oil" theory and the world's diminishing petroleum supplies, by U.S. Representative Roscoe G. Bartlett, the Republican of Maryland's Sixth District, on March 14, 2005, to the House of Representatives

Let us go back to the 1940s and the 1950s when a scientist by the name of M. King Hubbert, a geologist, was working for the Shell Oil Company. He was watching the discovery and the exploitation and final exhaustion of individual oil fields. He noticed that every oil field followed a very typical pattern. It was a little slow getting the oil out at first, and then it came very quickly and reached a maximum, and then it tailed off as it became more difficult to get the oil out of the ground.

This followed a bell curve. . . . Now, bell curves are very familiar in science, and in life, for that matter. If we look at people and how tall they are, we will have a few people down around 4½ or 5 feet and some up to 7½ feet; but the big mass fall in the middle, clustered around 5½ to 6 feet.

Looking at a yield of corn, a few farmers may get 50 bushels per acre, some may get 300, but the big mass today is somewhere around 200 bushels per acre for corn.

Hubbert noticed when the bell curve reached its peak, about half of the oil had been exhausted from the field. Being a scientist, he theorized if you added up a lot of little bell curves, you would get one big bell curve, and if he could know the amount of reserves of oil in the United States—and he was doing this in the 1940s and early 1950s—and could project how much more might be found, he could then predict when the United States would peak in its oil production.

Doing this analysis, he concluded that we would peak in our oil production in 1970. This curve is what is known as Hubbert's Curve. The peak of the curve is what is known as Hubbert's Peak. Sometimes this is called the "great rollover" because when you get to the top, you roll over and start down the other side. It is frequently called "peak oil." So peak oil for the United States occurred in 1970, and it is true that every year since then we have pumped less oil and found less oil. . . . Notice that the Alaska oil production was not the typical bell curve. It should have been, but a couple of things meant it could not be. One was it could not flow at all until we had a four-foot pipeline. So the fields were developed and they were waiting; then we got the pipeline on board, and it was filled with oil and oil started to flow, and Members see the rapid increase here. It could not flow any faster than through that four-foot pipe, and so it levels off at the top. We have pumped probably three-fourths of the oil in Prudhoe Bay.

Many people would like to open up ANWR [the Arctic National Wildlife Refuge]. ANWR has considerably less oil than Prudhoe Bay, so the contribution will be significantly less. I want to note on this chart we also have the red curve, which is the theoretical curve for the former Soviet Union. It is a nice bell curve, peaking a little higher—they have more reserves than we do—and later because we entered the industrial age with vigor before the Soviet Union was quite there. Notice what happened when they came apart; notice how precipitously it fell here. After they got things organized, the fall stopped and now they are producing more oil. As a matter of fact, we might see a little upsurge in this; but the general trend is still going to be down. . . .

We are, by the way, very good at finding oil now. We use 3D seismic detection techniques. The world has drilled, I think, about 5 million oil wells and I think we have drilled about 3 million of them in this country, so we have a pretty good idea of where oil is.

A couple of Congresses ago, I was privileged to chair the Energy Subcommittee on Science. One of the first things I wanted to do was to determine the dimensions of the problem. We held a couple of hearings and had the world experts in. Surprisingly, from the most pessimistic to the most optimistic, there was not much deviation in what the estimate is as to what the known reserves are out there. It is about 1,000 gigabarrels. That sounds like an awful lot of oil. But when you divide into that the amount of oil which we use, about 20 million barrels a day, and the amount of oil the rest of the world uses, about 60 million barrels a day, as a matter of fact, the total now is a bit over the 80 million that those two add up to. About 83½, I think. If you divide that into the 1,000 gigabarrels, you come out at about forty years of oil remaining in the world. That is pretty good. Because up until the Carter years, during the Carter years, in every decade we used as much oil as had been used in all of previous history. Let me repeat that, because that is startling. In every decade, we used as much oil as had been used in all of previous history. The reason for that, of course, was that we were on the upward side of this bell curve. . . . The Energy Information Agency says that we are going to keep on using more oil. . . . But that cannot be true. That cannot be true for a couple of reasons. We peaked in our discovery of oil way back here in the late sixties, about 1970. In our country it peaked much earlier than that, by the way. But the world is following several years behind us. . . . You cannot pump any more oil than you have found, quite obviously. If you have not found it, you cannot pump it.

Let me mention that M. King Hubbert looked at the world situation. He was joined by another scientist, Colin Campbell, who is still alive, an American citizen who lives in Scotland. Using M. King Hubbert's predictive techniques, [world production of] oil was predicted to reach a maximum in about 1995, without perturbations. But there were some perturbations. One of the perturbations was 1973, the Arab oil embargo. Other perturbations were the oil price shocks and a worldwide recession that reduced the demand for oil. And so the peak that might have occurred in 1995 will occur later. How much later? That is what we are looking at this evening. There is a lot of evidence that suggests that if not now, then very quickly we should see world production of oil peak.

What are the consequences? What are the consequences of this depletion? The remaining oil is harder to get. It requires greater energy investment, resulting in a lower return on energy invested. That is the energy-profit ratio, which is decreasing. When we started out, you put in one unit of energy and you could get thirty out. Then that fell off, and then we found a few more fields and we got really good at extracting oil with better techniques. It looked for a little while like it was going up, but look what happened. It falls off to where it would have come anyhow if this curve had simply gone down. This is an inevitable consequence of pumping a field.

Lower profits are not the only concern. When more energy is required to extract it than is contained in the recovered oil, that is, when this ratio is less than 1, notice, we are over there at about 1984, we have got to get now another twenty years, I am not quite sure where we are now when you plot that day. We are getting very close to the unit it takes as much energy to get the oil out as you get out of the oil. It may still seem profitable from a monetary perspective, but when you are using more energy to get oil out of the ground than you are getting out of the oil, then clearly you need to leave it there when we reach that point. . . . .

What is the current U.S. status? One barrel of oil, forty-two gallons of oil, equals the productivity of 25,000 man-hours. That is the equivalent of having sixty dedicated servants that do nothing but work for someone. We can get a little better real-life example of this. A gallon of gas will drive a three-ton SUV, and some of those are better than others, and let us say it takes it twenty minutes, which some will but most will not. Most are around ten. But let us say one gallon of gas will take a three-ton SUV 20 miles at sixty miles an hour down the road. That is just one little gallon of gas, which, by the way, is still cheaper than water. We pay more for water in the grocery store than we pay for gas at $2 a gallon at the pump, added up.

How long would it take one to push their three-ton SUV the equivalent of sixty miles an hour, twenty miles down the road? To get some idea of the energy density in these fossil fuels, there is just nothing out there in the alternatives that have anything like this energy density. There are some potentials, nuclear, and we will talk about those in a little bit. But of the general renewables, there is nothing out there with that kind of density. So this curve is likely to be much lower than this curve; and notice that if it is, in fact, going to be renewable, it cannot go to an unrealistic height. There is only so much wood to cut. Easter Island had that experience. When they cut the last tree, they totally changed the ecology.

The Bible talks about the large clusters of grapes and the honey and so forth that they found when the spies went out. That now is a desert. The Cedars of Lebanon, the grand Cedars of Lebanon that built the temple, that is now largely a desert. Why is it a desert? Because they cut the trees, they changed the environment, they changed the climate. So obviously this line has to be a reasonable sustainable level. It just cannot go on forever.

The challenge, then, is to reduce consumption ultimately to a level that cannot be sustained indefinitely without succumbing to Jevons Paradox. [The Jevons Paradox is named for William Stanley Jevons, who theorized in the 1860s in England that when technology becomes more energy-efficient, the result can be that total consumption of that resource—in that case, coal—increases because the energy savings inspires growth.]

How do we buy time, the time that we will need to make the transition to sustainability? Obviously, there are only two things that we can do to buy time. One is to conserve, and the other is to be more efficient. And the gentleman from Maryland (Mr. Gilchrest) mentioned our increasing efficiency. We have done a great job. Our refrigerators today are probably twice as efficient as they were twenty or thirty years ago. But instead of a little refrigerator, we have a big one. Instead of one, we may have two. So I will bet we are using as much electricity in our refrigeration as we ever used.

Conservation, we can do that. Remember several years ago when there were brownouts, blackouts in California and we were predicting, boy, the next year is really going to be rough? Do the

Members know why it was not and we did not see any headlines about blackouts in California? Because knowing that there was a problem, the Californians, without anybody telling them they had to, voluntarily reduced their electricity consumption by 11%. That is pretty significant. And that avoided the rolling blackouts or brownouts.

And, finally, we must commit to major investments in alternatives, especially as efficiencies improve. This must ultimately lead to the ability to do everything within the capability of renewable resources. If we have got a solar breeder—this shows a picture of a solar breeder. That, by the way, is about five miles from my home. It was built by Solarex, and it is a sign of the times. Mr. Speaker, this is now owned by BP. They know that oil is not forever. They are now the world's second-largest producer of solar panels.

A few years ago, the largest buyer of solar panels in the world, and I do not know if that is true today, but a few years ago it was Saudi Arabia. Why would Saudi Arabia, with the most oil in the world, be the biggest purchaser of solar panels in the world? The reasons are very simple. These are not dumb people, and they figured out that solar panels were better for them in producing electricity than oil because they had widely distributed communities that were very small. Electrons in a wire are very different than oil in a pipeline. Put a gallon of oil in a pipeline up at Prudhoe Bay, and a gallon will come out where it goes on the ship. If we put electrons in a line which is long enough, nothing will come out in the other end. It is called line loss.

And they knew that in their small communities, widely distributed, with the enormous line losses they had from big plants, that they would be better off with distributed production.

By the way, just a hint to our people who are concerned with homeland security—the more distributed production we have, the less vulnerable we are going to be to terrorist attacks on our power infrastructure.

Transition to sustainability will not happen if left applying market forces alone. Everyone must be part of the effort or Jevons Paradox will prevail. If only our country tries to do it and nobody else helps, we will just put off the day when we must make the transition, and it will be even more difficult. The market will, indeed, signal the arrival of peak oil. To wait until it does, however, is like waiting until we see a tsunami: by then it may be too late to do anything.

We now are doing a lot of talking here in the Congress and fortunately across the country about Social Security, and it is a big problem. But I tell the Members if the problem of Social Security is equivalent to the tidal wave produced by the hurricane, then this peak oil problem is equivalent to the tsunami. The impact and the consequences are going to be enormously greater than the impact and the consequences of Social Security or Medicare or those two put together.

It will take a sustained, conscious, coordinated national—and even international—effort. If everybody is not working together and buying time by conserving and being efficient and using wisely that time we bought, then all we do is put off the inevitable.

The hydroelectric and nuclear power industries did not arise spontaneously from market forces alone. They were the product of a purposeful partnership of public and private entities focused on the public good. This is what we have to do relative to alternatives.

As I mentioned, California solved their energy crisis by voluntarily reducing their demand for electricity. Time, capital, and energy resources are all finite. We have only so much time until it would be too late to avoid a real problem. Capital is limited and energy resources are certainly limited.

This time it will not be like the seventies. The big difference between now and the seventies is that in the seventies, we were just going up this curve; we were nowhere near the top of the curve, so there was always the ability to expand, to surge. If, in fact, we are now at peak oil, there is no such ability remaining.

CHAPTER TWO

Demystifying Solar Energy

During the recent years of war and unrest in the Middle East, the home of most of the world's oil reserves, the idea of using solar energy has started to come back. The U.S. Congress has approved drilling for what might be not much oil in the Arctic National Wildlife Refuge. These politically tense enterprises to find more oil, along with high electricity rates, air pollution, and the changing climate, have all made people begin to ask if there's a better way to make power.

It takes you back—to President Jimmy Carter.

In April 1977, in the midst of the energy crisis, President Jimmy Carter gave a speech beseeching the public to learn to get away from oil and promoting the need to conserve energy and find alternatives. Today, his words still sound prophetic rather than nostalgic. Even though political leaders still tell Americans to conserve energy at home, most of Carter's recommendations didn't happen. By the 1990s and 2000s, America found itself vulnerable to oil-producing countries in the midst of Middle East unrest. Three decades later, Carter's 1977 speech still lays out untested notions of dealing with energy shortages.

Here are his most memorable statements from that speech:

We must not be selfish or timid if we hope to have a decent world for our children and grandchildren.

We simply must balance our demand for energy with our rapidly shrinking resources. By acting now, we can control our future instead of letting the future control us.

Two days from now, I will present my energy proposals to the Congress. . . . Many of these proposals will be unpopular. Some will cause you to put up with inconveniences and to make sacrifices.

The most important thing about these proposals is that the alternative may be a national catastrophe. Further delay can affect our strength and our power as a nation.

Our decision about energy will test the character of the American people and the ability of the President and the Congress to govern. This difficult effort will be the "moral equivalent of war"—except that we will be uniting our efforts to build and not destroy.

I know that some of you may doubt that we face real energy shortages. The 1973 gasoline lines are gone, and our homes are warm again. But our energy problem is worse tonight than it was in 1973 or a few weeks ago in the dead of winter. It is worse because more waste has occurred, and more time has passed by without our planning for the future. And it will get worse every day until we act.[1]

TO GO SOLAR, YOU MUST USE LESS ENERGY

When Carter went on to lay out the principles of his energy policy, he linked the growth of solar technology to learning to use less electricity. Without one, the other isn't possible. In the late 1970s, the country would begin to explore alternative energy technologies that could be produced at home. The cornerstone of the policy would be, "to reduce the demand through conservation. Our emphasis on conservation is a clear difference between this plan and others which merely encouraged crash production efforts. Conservation is the quickest, cheapest, most practical source of energy." Carter's words were rare for a leader not because he asked each citizen to look inward and cut personal energy use (many presidents have said the same thing, with varying amounts of attention from the populace) but because he assumed that the country would have to brace itself for *not* finding enough oil to support the way we'd been living.

Two years later, in 1979, Carter tried to set an example when he ordered a solar-powered hot water heating system placed on the roof of the White House staff kitchen. The government had to hire a contractor from Vermont to install the panels because no one in Washington knew how. The man spent that April installing 320 panels, each measuring four-by-eight feet, on the White House kitchen roof. The system heated some of the water for the staff kitchens, where several hundred employees ate.[2]

President Carter wanted solar energy to make up 20% of the country's power by 2000. By 2004, the sun, combined with other alternative sources such as geothermal heat, made up less than 3% of the country's power.[3]

People who installed solar-powered systems in their houses during the Carter years received federal tax reductions. Americans spent $171 million on solar equipment in 1979. By 1981, they had spent almost $679 million (the government reimbursed up to 40% of their costs).

After Ronald Reagan became president in 1980, world markets and domestic attitudes changed. Oil prices dropped, and solar energy seemed something for true-believer homesteaders. In 1981, Reagan's administration began to cut back solar programs. In 1985, Carter's solar tax credits expired. Between July 1985 and July 1986, the price of home heating oil went from $1.04 a gallon to 66¢. The number of solar equipment manufacturers dropped from about 200 in the late 1970s to about 30 in 1985.

Sometime later, Carter's White House panels stopped functioning. In 1986, a roof-repair crew took them down, and the White House announced they would not be put back. The news appeared in newspapers as an Associated Press brief, in which an unnamed government official said, "Putting them back up would be very unwise, based on cost."

THE WHITE HOUSE SOLAR PANELS: RELICS

For years after, the practice of gathering sunlight for domestic heat seemed to go along with the back-to-the-landers eating crunchy granola. From 1986 to 1991, Jimmy Carter's panels sat in a giant storage area in suburban Virginia. Then Peter Marbach, a development director trying to get Unity College in Maine some national attention, heard about the panels. He thought they were neither junk nor symbols of a mistaken energy policy. Peter Marbach decided to buy the panels and to put them into use at Unity College.

"I just started making phone calls, and then I got the idea to write to Jimmy Carter and tell him what we were trying to do," said Marbach, who today is a photographer living in Oregon. "He wrote back amazingly fast. He sent back the letter I sent him and put a handwritten note on top: 'It would please me to see these panels restored. Good luck.' "

Marbach removed the seats from the school basketball team's old bus, drove it down to Virginia, paid a few hundred dollars, and loaded the panels himself. When he got back, he raised money to install them. Even the most modern solar collectors for hot water systems require some kind of a backup system to complete the job. Carter's vintage 1979 system only took the chill off water going into the oil-fired hot water heater for Unity's meals, thereby cutting the fuel bill slightly. By doing only that, the panels did exactly what they were designed to do. For several years, they did their job—until 1998, when a bad ice storm damaged the panels. For more than three years, they sat there. The physical plant director, Roger Duval, found a company in Portland that was willing to restore them for $1,400.

By 2005, Unity College had taken the panels off-line. They needed repairs. A professor was looking into donating one of the panels to the Smithsonian, while the college hoped to find sponsors to donate money to restore the panels as artifacts. They are artifacts, but they also symbolize the hope of a technology that hasn't yet reached its potential. Marbach seemed an unlikely archaeologist when he rescued a piece of history. Perhaps heating systems like this do belong in museums—or perhaps not. Perhaps Peter Marbach was just a master recycler. What he did do as he rescued the panels was to bring back into the public consciousness these solar energy artifacts that started out symbolizing hope and ended up forgotten objects.

Carter believed that his solar panels would become common around America. Carter's panels look like Cro-Magnon tools next to what we have today. But don't laugh at President Carter's panels. Salute the memory.

THE TECHNOLOGY

Solar electricity is the quietest form of making energy. There are two different methods of doing so. The first, the newest incarnations of Jimmy Carter's first panels, heat water. **Solar thermal collectors,** which heat hot water, use pipes filled with solutions similar to antifreeze. These have greatly improved since the Carter administration. The pipes run from the solar panels on the roof to a tank where, like coils, they warm the water. The earliest versions of these systems went up around the country starting in 1973 in response to the first Arab oil embargo. These panels marked the birth of the modern solar industry. When another embargo pinched supplies in 1979, more solar companies formed. Between 1973 and 1979, the number of solar collector manufacturers went from 45 to 225. The federal government, and many state governments, offered financial help for solar collector buyers.[4] Today's solar thermal collectors can pay for themselves in four to eight years, according to the Worldwatch Institute.[5]

The **photovoltaic (PV) panel,** which collects sunlight and converts it to electricity, absorbs sunlight into a semiconductor material, usually silicon. Silicon is the third most common element in the Earth's crust behind aluminum and oxygen. The resulting electron activity is harnessed into energy through wires at the panel's back. The sun hits the solar photovoltaic panel, or module, each of which contains rows of *cells*—often thirty-six of them to a panel. (For an explanation of the physics of this, see the boxed section, "How Solar Photovoltaic Cells Work" on page 43.)

The solar-collected energy travels down the wires to your fuse box and eventually to your lights and appliances, if you are using them. If you don't need the power just then, it goes into batteries (if you have batteries) that store the power until it's needed, or it goes through wires out to the street and to the regional power grid, if you are grid-connected.

Regardless of whether it's stored, the energy must flow through another box, the *inverter*, before it can power appliances and lights. The inverter converts the powerful DC power to alternating current (or AC) power, which runs everything electrical in the United States. Some appliances can run directly off DC power collected in PV cells, if they are designed for it.

If your system stores electricity for later use in batteries, they usually can save enough power for a weeklong supply or more, depending on the size of the system. More common with today's new solar PV systems is to tie the system to the grid—since most rebate programs require this. When you tie to the grid, you do not store power unless you also invest in a battery bank. Grid-tied systems send unneeded power out of the house to electricity customers elsewhere. When excess power the house doesn't need goes out to the grid, the meter runs backward. This usually happens in the middle of a sunny day, when no one is home. The utility company pays the homeowner for the power at wholesale rates. You won't get rich off selling sun to the utility, but many people who do this have electric bills so low they seem caught in a time warp.

PRACTICALITY SETS IN

Only a few years ago, almost no one knew a solar power user. That is starting to change. A few years ago, with not much fanfare, President George W. Bush's administration installed a set of solar photovoltaic panels on a National Park Service building on the White House grounds. While this move didn't grow out of Bush's personal appeal to the country in the way the first White House panels grew out of Carter's, the installation does prove that solar panels are simply too sensible not to use in such places. Look at highway message signs, portable construction equipment, and marker lights in your neighbor's garden and you will see solar photovoltaic panels. Look on the roof of the occasional house. Those mirrored rectangular panels aren't some strange decoration. They are solar collectors. Any ordinary person can begin to use these.

Production of solar equipment has grown quickly in the past few years. The Worldwatch Institute reports that worldwide production of photovoltaic cells was roughly 1,200 megawatts in 2004, which was 58% more than in 2003. Production of these panels doubled in a two-year period. In 2004, the country that appeared to be ahead of other countries in photovoltaic production was Japan, where the government has pushed for this technology and where 160,000 houses are powered with photovoltaics. Worldwatch says that the market for solar thermal collectors—used for water heaters or building heat—grew by 50% between 2001 and 2004 on a worldwide basis, serving about 32 million households (not counting swimming pool heaters). Solar hot water heaters are not big in the United States at the moment. Here, 98% of the solar hot water heaters are used for pools. That leaves room for a lot of growth.[6]

THE REBATES ARRIVE

Solar technology is on the rise, but it hasn't moved into the mainstream. Why? In the United States, until 2004 and 2005, the reasons were all cost related. Photovoltaic systems are expensive, or about $50,000 for a system large enough to power a modest house. But a few years ago, many states began offering rebates that cover a good chunk of the cost of photovoltaic systems and solar thermal systems. These rebates have made solar affordable to the middle class for the first time since the incentives of the Carter years (see the sidebar on page 40).

Because solar is still a new technology, and because it requires conservation, some people might feel reluctant to try it. But if a solar photovoltaic system hooks into the power grid, backup power is always available. Still, solar panel users remain rare people who are motivated to conserve energy. The solar users I have met talk about their conservation ethic. They don't want to have to resort to buying too much electricity from the grid—especially while they are still paying for the solar panels. They want to make it work. When they bought the panels, they also bought into a way of life. They made a commitment to spend more money than most to provide basic utilities, and they continually have to take steps, every day, to live differently at home—by using less power.

They have acted on their belief that the time has come when ordinary Americans will start looking at the sun somewhere other than at the beach. Many Americans pay little attention to the sun beyond its availability for suntanning. An artist I know in Old Saybrook, Connecticut, spent a year painting sunrises. One of the days happened to be the first day of 2000. When he got to the shore of the Connecticut River, he found a crowd of people looking to the east, waiting with him for the sunrise. One of them suggested that after he finished his painting, he might like to take a drive around to a town beach on Long Island Sound, a few miles away. He headed over there to find a crowd of people sitting patiently, waiting for the sun to rise from the southwest.

GETTING STARTED WITH SOLAR

If you plan to harness the abundant stores of energy from the sun that hit most regions of the Northern Hemisphere, be sure you know which direction is south. If the roof does not face the right direction, you can affix panels to poles set wherever they need to be. Then, consider the funds. Does your state offer incentives or rebates? (See the sidebar, page 40.) Remember that in most cases, for every watt a solar panel generates, it costs roughly $10 in initial investment. Thus, 1,000 watts of power, or 1 kilowatt, would cost about $10,000. Generating 4 kilowatts, or enough to power a fairly conservation-savvy household, would cost roughly $40,000.[7]

The average electricity use in my home state of Connecticut is about five times that amount, but anyone who goes solar quickly gets down to the lower level by incorporating major conservation moves into their habits. (See chapters 8 to 10 for more.)

As of this writing, twenty-three states now offer rebates for new solar energy installations. The rebates cut the cost in half in my state, making it an attractive idea. In New Jersey, the state pays for 70% of solar PV installations. (For details, see the Appendix.) The systems eligible for rebates must tie into the electric power grid so that any excess power drawn in can go out to the street lines to be used somewhere else. As long as the system provides 3 to 5 kilowatts a day, it will run backward during sunny times when the household needs little power.

STARTING SMALL

No one needs to try to power an entire household on solar panels. You can start very small, although to do so will feel like a hobby. It's possible to buy a single 100-watt panel for about $750, give or take a few hundred—but that doesn't include other equipment you need to hook up to the grid. (Remember, if you plan to take advantage of state rebate programs, hooking up to the grid is a requirement of these incentives that have made solar panels so much more afford-able in recent years.) Gail Burrington, owner of Burrington's Solar Edge in Windsor Locks, Connecticut, does not recommend that you go solar on such a small scale. According to Burrington, it would not be worth the cost to provide so little electricity for your house.[8]

For about $4,600, she says, you can get a 480-watt system of a few panels with necessary equipment. If you prefer not to install a system that would tie into the power grid and just want to do something small to cut your energy use, you can buy, for example, sump pumps for about $400 that run off a single solar panel or attic fans that run entirely on solar. You can buy yard lights with solar panels

Solar panels in the tops of these lights illuminate a path after dark.

in the top. You can rig up a solar panel to any single appliance, too, without tying into the grid.

The equipment is expensive. But so are cars, trips to Disney World, jewelry, houses, and cruise vacations—and all of those things don't reduce greenhouse gas emissions. It takes between fifteen and thirty years to recoup the financial cost of most systems—depending on the size of the system, electric rates, and whether a rebate covers part of the cost. But the environmental benefits begin immediately when you begin producing clean energy that doesn't pollute the air. Many objects for which we pay dearly depreciate from the moment we buy them. The Connecticut Clean Energy Fund explains in its guide for consumers that, "buying a PV system is like paying years of electric bills up front. You'll probably appreciate the reduction in your monthly electric bills, but the initial expense may be significant. Improved manufacturing has reduced the cost of PV equipment to less than 1 % of what it was in the 1970s, but the cost amortized over the life of the system is still about 25 cents per kilowatt-hour. This cost is roughly twice the direct retail price that most Connecticut residents now pay for electricity from their utilities."[9]

One of the most inexpensive and sensible ways to light the edges of paths and driveways is the solar-powered driveway light. We have some that cost about $10 apiece at a home store, and at about $25 and up, you can buy sturdier ones that look quite nice.

If you dislike the look of solar PV panels on your roof, consider roofing shingles that double as solar panels. At least two companies are producing these now. The downside is that they have been reported to be less efficient than the thicker PV panels.

Another way to start small is to invest in solar-powered appliances, each attached to individual solar panels that send direct current to the appliance. (No inverter to convert to alternating current is necessary, since these don't connect to the household electrical system.)

One of the most logical and useful solar-powered appliances is the solar-powered attic fan, also called an attic vent. It looks like a rectangular solar panel on the roof, but it includes a fan that blows hot air out of the house. The fan receives the most power from the solar unit when the house needs the fan the most—on hot, sunny days. These fans typically cost in the hundreds of dollars.

Or try a solar-powered sump pump, which won't have to rely on the electricity supply of the house that might shut down during a flood.

Individual solar panels hook up to power laptop computers and other communication devices for field work or travel. Call any solar dealer to ask about these products, or search on the Web to learn more. Direct-current solar appliances even turn up on eBay.

A solar system that would provide the amount of power most Americans use now would have to be very large—too large to be practical. Solar power in enough quantity can comfortably provide for needs, but it can't provide for the kind of waste Americans take for granted. So you have to learn to turn off lights and power strips, unplug appliances that do not run off power strips, and stop using unnecessary electric appliances. Heating and cooling use the most energy. With a solar PV system, you'd need to heat your water with propane or a separate solar hot water system. You'd also need to cut back on cooling. Start by buying a low-energy refrigerator. Read about the history of conservation and tips for saving energy in chapters 8, 9, and 10.

The Consortium for Advanced Residential Buildings (CARB), a program of the Department of Energy, has determined that energy savings from solar panels can vary greatly from house to house based on how carefully people conserve. In California in 2003, a construction company built a group of energy-efficient houses in Sacramento. The utility, Sacramento Municipal Utility District, offered solar systems to builders at a discount in order to encourage a lower electricity use. The built-in roof panels generated 3.3 kilowatt-hours, or theoretically enough to power the homes without backup power from the grid. The utility announced that the goal was for the houses to use zero net electricity throughout the year—in other words, to use only the sun. Throughout 2004, the utility kept track of electricity use at eleven of the houses. Only two of the houses reached the goal. The rest used varying amounts of added electricity above and beyond the solar systems.

The discrepancies showed that "the ultimate responsibility in attaining 'zero energy' lies with the user," as CARB reported in a newsletter.[10] It's up to us to make this work.

ONE FAMILY'S EXPERIENCE

In 2003, Peter Markow, a chemistry professor at St. Joseph's College in West Hartford, Connecticut, and his wife, Claire, decided to invest in a solar photovoltaic system for his house in Tolland, where they live with their son and daughter. They refinanced the house (this was before his state offered rebates) and located a clearing at the back of their property where they could mount the forty-eight 100-watt panels, which cost $51,000. "We have no real south-facing roof, so we mounted them on metal poles on concrete tubes going down four feet," he says. "We put them up in November 2003. In 2004, 81% of all our electricity needs came from the sun." As good as that was, he notes that the saleswoman had optimistically predicted that 100% of their needs would be fulfilled by the panels. It is true that occasionally, for short periods, the panels gave them much more than they need. April 2005, for example, was an unusually sunny month with almost no rain. According to a computer program Peter monitors daily, the system provided 121% of the Markow family's electricity that month. (Of course, the amount above 100% went out onto the power grid.)

Conserving electricity is not difficult, he says. They switched to compact fluorescent bulbs, which use much less energy than regular bulbs. The house is well insulated. (Note that they use an oil furnace.) They close windows in the summer to keep the night's cool air inside the house. The attic is insulated, holding in heat in the winter and cool air in the summer.

"I was doing this because I wanted to do it," he says. "I want to show the world that this is doable—right here in Connecticut." The truth is that solar PV panels operate better in cool temperatures, when electrons move off the silicon more efficiently.

Because the Markows made their move to solar without the benefit of government rebates, they would have to live to be biblically old to recoup their financial investment in the panels. Connecticut has since instituted a rebate program that funds about half of the cost of most systems. Markow estimates that for the year 2004, they spent $50 on electric bills and generated power through the sun that would have cost them $550—for a net savings of $500 for one year. Markow doesn't care that their move to alternative energy isn't going to make them money. He didn't do it for the money, but the family found ways to make the investment sensibly. They refinanced their mortgage from 7.7% to 5.5% and wrapped the solar cost into it. "The aspect I'd like to promote is: What's the environmental benefit of doing this, and the environmental *cost* of our energy use." Using his computer program, which records the total amount of energy the panels bring in (whether it goes out to the grid or not), Markow is producing detailed records of his foray into alternative energy. (See chart, page 44.)[11]

States Offering Financial Assistance to Buy Solar

For complete details, see the Appendix

Arizona	Nevada
California	New Jersey
Colorado	New York
Connecticut	Oregon
Delaware	Pennsylvania
Florida	Rhode Island
Hawaii	South Carolina
Illinois	Texas
Maryland	Washington
Massachusetts	Wisconsin
Michigan	Wyoming
Minnesota	

The following chart shows that the Connecticut family's 4-kilowatt solar array generates the majority of the electricity they need. Because this is a grid-connected system, their costs and savings must consider the difference between what the power company pays them for excess power and what they must buy during dark or very cloudy periods.

Never forget that grid-tied solar systems do not store excess solar power at the house for later use. During the sunniest times of day, power the house doesn't use immediately flows out to the power grid. After dark, any electricity they need flows in from the grid, and they must pay for that power.

This chart is based on the family's records in 2004, including the price of electricity at that time, which, including service charges, fluctuated between 13¢ and 14¢ per kilowatt-hour. Most months, they spent slightly more for power than they saved by making their own, but as they learn to conserve at crucial times of the day, their savings could increase.

The state of Connecticut was not paying rebates when the Markows put in their system, but typically, a system subsidized by a rebate will pay itself off in about twenty years. The Markows paid full freight for their system and acknowledge they won't pay it off. In most months, too, they paid out more for power than they took in.

Don't think of this as a business, though. The Markows paid the power company only $597.59 for the whole year. If they had had to buy all of their power from the grid, that would have cost them more than $2,380.

continued

Markow Family's Solar Electric Production and Savings

Month	Solar kilowatt hours the Markows produced	Solar kilowatt hours they used at home (the rest, they sold to the grid)	Power the Markows bought from Connecticut Light & Power, in kilowatt-hours	Amount they paid the power company	Money saved (Money spent)
January	379	104	397	$52.64	($10.69)
February	507	148	327	$44.89	$9.54
March	378	134	367	$49.32	($8.48)
April	495	152	324	$44.56	$8.60
May	506	144	265	$38.03	$12.86
June	478	164	292	$41.03	$10.71
July	451	259	452	$58.73	($8.81)
August	487	201	369	$49.54	$4.37
September	386	173	482	$62.05	($19.32)
October	353	112	335	$45.77	($6.58)
November	344	104	369	$49.54	($11.15)
December	273	97	477	$61.49	($31.16)
Total	5037	1792	4456	$597.59	($50.11)

SOURCE: Peter Markow, who uses this chart in his classes at St. Joseph's College in West Hartford.

How Solar Photovoltaic Cells Work

Solar photovoltaics funnel energy through a semiconductor to wires. The way they work is rarely explained to the unknowing public. This description by my physics teacher husband, Nat Eddy, began as a discussion and grew into this.

Solar photovoltaic panels use light to produce electricity. They are generally made of silicon, which is a semiconductor. Semiconductors hang on to their electrons more tightly than electrical conductors like metals do, but less tightly than insulators. So under some circumstances they will conduct electricity, and under others they will not.

This is important, because the way they create an electrical current is that their electrons are held loosely enough that they can be knocked off when light falls on them (creating an area of positive charge), but held tightly enough that they do not migrate easily through the material to equalize the distribution of charges. This means that there is a potential (or voltage) difference between the front and the back of the silicon, and if a conductive path were made from front to back, current would flow to equalize the charges.

Silicon alone wouldn't be a very useful source of electrical current. The cells are not very efficient, so there aren't a whole lot of electrons being knocked off. So to be useful, photovoltaics must have a structure that allows them to produce and maintain a reasonably large voltage. Manufacturers "dope" the silicon, which means that they add to the silicon small amounts of other materials that have either more outer electrons, or fewer, than silicon has.

This means there is a source of extra electrons, or a lack of electrons (called holes), relative to the atoms of the silicon. The extra electrons can jump from atom to atom, and so can the holes, since when an electron from the silicon jumps into the hole, it creates a hole in the atom it left, which another electron can fill, and so on. So the doped silicon can conduct a current, by either electrons or holes being passed from atom to atom. If the doping provides extra electrons (which are negatively charged), it is called *N-type*, and if it provides holes (which means a missing electron, so the atom is positively charged), it is called *P-type*.

In a photovoltaic cell, a thin P-type layer is deposited on top of an N-type layer (or vice versa). Where the layers contact each other, the extra N-type electrons immediately fill in the holes in the P-type and neutralize or deplete each other. But deeper in the layers, away from the boundary, the charges— electrons and holes—attract each other. They migrate and cross over to the other layer. This means that the N-type layer becomes somewhat positively charged because holes have migrated over, and the P-type layer negatively charged because electrons have migrated.

As the charges increase, the layers become less and less attractive to further charges, and eventually, migration ceases and equilibrium is established. Note that there is a potential difference between the layers, so a voltage has been established.

If light now falls on the photovoltaic cell, it will pass through the very thin P-type layer and knock off electrons from the N-type layer. It might seem that the electrons ought to jump into holes in the P-type layer, but remember—that layer has now become negatively charged, so instead, the electrons migrate away to the back of the N-type layer, where there is a metal backing. Electrons accumulate on the backing, creating a negative charge there.

Meanwhile, the holes created when the electrons were knocked off migrate to the negatively charged P layer. There, they diminish the negative charge on that layer, functionally creating a relative positive charge.

If the photovoltaic cell were not part of an electrical circuit, as the charges on the layers increased, it would become harder and harder for more electrons and holes to migrate, and equilibrium would again be established. But if the cell is made part of a circuit, the accumulated charges will be able to move off the cell through the circuit, and as long as light falls on the cell, electrons and holes will keep being created and migrating, maintaining a continuous potential (or voltage) difference, so that electric current will continue to flow.

CHAPTER THREE

Wind Generators at Home

The first time I encountered wind power close-up
was in the fall of 2003 in the White Mountains of New Hampshire,
where I had just spent the night at the Galehead Hut, a backcountry
cabin with bunks and meals. Walking outside in the morning, I heard
a whirring, buzzing sound. I looked up and saw a tiny periscope-
shaped object with a moving propeller perched on the roof peak. Its
tiny propeller whirred so fast that it blurred as it collected energy to,
it turned out, power the lights. The Appalachian Mountain Club,
which operates these hikers' outposts, has started using clean energy
where possible. From their perches at more than 3,500 feet above sea
level, these wind turbines can collect enough power, along with solar
photovoltaic panels, to run all of the hut lights. (The lights are turned
off every night at 9:30 P.M. The extra power collected is stored in batteries.) Until you have seen a wind-gathering contraption you might
not appreciate the beauty of using a constant source of power. Get
used to the idea. It's coming. Modern civilization had until recently
ignored wind because petroleum has provided the inexpensive lifeline.

You can use wind to make your electricity. You won't be able to
power much of your house with the tiny ones, and they won't work well
at the height of most rooftops in America unless, as one consultant told

me, all you want is to power the brake lights of your car. Instead, you will need a turbine with blades twenty feet in diameter that sit atop a tall tower away from the house.

This basic technology isn't new, but until a few years ago the idea inspired little interest. In the 1970s a researcher described an already advanced wind power technology in a textbook, noting, "Scarcely anyone has paid any real attention to the moral or ethical consideration involved in this, plus the next few generations burning up all the remaining fossil fuels and raising accumulated radioactivity far above the natural background level; many nations are now willing to at least discuss these things, but very little action has yet been taken." The researcher noted that a "mature" wind technology already was in place and that "assembly line production of components could start in a relatively short time. Wind power could impact the United States energy market starting in as few as four years if treated as a national priority goal." Of course, this did not happen.

It was 1973 when William E. Heronemus, professor of civil engineering at the University of Massachusetts, wrote those words. Even he seemed ready for the public to reject wind when he noted that if people thought that wind generators looked ugly, then "they cannot be used." His remarks seem to have predicted the kind of reluctant fear that has greeted many large wind farm proposals—most publicly, one proposed for the Atlantic Ocean off Nantucket. According to the developer, Energy Management Inc., the Cape Wind project consists of 130 wind turbines with a maximum output of 420 megawatts. The turbines would stand on Horseshoe Shoal, five miles offshore. The shoal is very shallow but most of it is usually submerged. Cape Wind says that these turbines should produce three-quarters of the energy needed on Cape Cod, Martha's Vineyard, and Nantucket. Even environmentalists and elected officials have argued against so many blades turning in the seashore air space. The battles could go on until 2009, when the company hopes to begin making power.

Yet in its infancy, the wind power industry has done better on a utility scale than on a backyard scale. The wind industry installed 389 megawatts of capacity in 2004, giving the United States an installed base of 6,740 megawatts in thirty states. Developers were hurrying to build up to 2,500 megawatts of new wind projects before the end of 2005, when a tax credit was set to expire.[1] The American Wind Energy Association predicts that wind energy will provide 6% of the power in the United States by 2020.

Harnessing wind for power goes back to the beginning of human history, with sailing ships. In the twelfth century, about 10,000 windmills ground grain and pumped water in western Europe. For most of the last century, though, windmills have remained an historic relic. Only a few years ago, most people had never heard of wind power. People tended to associate it with windmills in oil paintings of seventeenth-century Holland. Today most wind power projects are large ones that send wind power through transmission lines from the windiest parts of the country, such as the Dakotas.

Wind power's undeniable environmental benefits butt against people's shock and resistance when they learn the height at which a wind turbine must turn in order to work. People who live near proposed wind farms here and abroad have protested the look of them. Most turbines are mounted on poles hundreds of feet tall. The reactions are explosive. In May 2005, 350 residents of rural Highland County in western Virginia flocked to a hearing on the state's first proposed wind farm. A retired turkey farmer sought to build nineteen wind turbines, 400 feet from base to top, on a ridge, generating 39 megawatts of power and more than $170,000 a year in tax revenues. Most of the county's residents signed a petition against the plan on the basis of how it would look. Almost everyone who spoke that night was against it (one person called it "a crime against nature"), and the hearing went until 2:30 A.M.[2]

The individual wind power gatherer faces fewer constraints. While utility-scale projects struggle to move forward, in many windy areas, residential-sized projects aren't even a dream yet. Anyplace where enough wind blows, property owners may consider running their own power off a single wind generator. As with solar power, you can take steps now and buy a wind power system. Beware: they are expensive and won't provide all the power you'll need—unless you have a lot of wind and enough room for a large unit. You must spend several thousand dollars for even the smallest of turbines. On the other hand, the payback time can be faster than solar. You don't have to wait for the country to sort out how to make wind technology mainstream. You can begin that transition at your place.

NECESSARY CONDITIONS

A house is ideal for an off-grid wind system if the wind in the area blows at an average annual speed of at least nine miles per hour. If your site is remote and would cost $15,000 or more per mile to connect to the grid, you're in an even better position. For a wind system that sells extra power back to the utility, the experts suggest that your annual wind speed reach at least ten miles per hour. High electric rates, rebates from the state, and friendly building codes, where available, help justify and reduce the dollars you'd spend. For instance, if you live in a place such as southern California where electricity rates are high, if the utility offers rebates (as California does), and if the building codes allow wind turbines, all of this can make the choice seem right almost immediately. Experts suggest that you own about an acre of land so you can erect a wind tower away from your house and the neighbors. Energy experts say that most residential wind customers must use larger turbines that sit atop tall towers that are at least sixty feet high. In order for wind to do the whole job for your house, you can't rely on one of those cute rooftop periscope-shaped turbines like the ones I saw in the White Mountains. Rooftop mini-generators must be in high-elevation locales, like the high-mountain huts in New Hampshire, or in ski huts in Colorado. I asked Mick Sagrillo, a wind energy consultant in Forestville, Wisconsin, with two decades' experience, about using a rooftop turbine. "No. You don't put wind generators on your roof," he said. "These are toys. A family of four is going to light a taillight bulb with one of those." Sagrillo explains that the principles of fluid dynamics dictate that the closer you are to the surface of the Earth, the stronger the ground drag (or interference) is, which slows the prevailing wind speed. The greatest decrease in drag happens between the ground and sixty feet up.

Above all, you must live in a place where the wind blows steadily and strong on the average. Wind power on the small scale is a great choice in windy parts of the country—and a dubious one in other places. If you live in North Dakota, South Dakota, Montana, Kansas, or Texas—the windiest places in the United States—consider using wind. The next fifteen windiest states after these, from windiest to least windy, are: Nebraska, Wyoming, Oklahoma, Minnesota, Iowa, Colorado, New Mexico, Idaho, Michigan, New York, Illinois, California, Wisconsin, Maine, and Missouri.[3]

HOW THEY WORK

Modern wind turbines look a little like propellers, with thin blades designed to move faster than the speed of the wind. The blades are connected to a magnet generator that turns to make power. Like solar power, this energy starts out as direct current that is converted to alternating current through an inverter.[4]

When the wind blows, the three-blade rotors start turning. The faster the wind, the faster the rotors turn. The higher off the ground the rotor is, the faster the wind that turns it. The larger the blades, the more electricity they produce. The contraption automatically turns sideways in very high winds to avoid destruction; it still produces electricity. A typical roof model, producing perhaps 1 kilowatt, measures 7.2 feet in diameter and begins turning when the wind reaches 6.7 miles per hour. A typical large pole-mounted turbine with three blades 8.2 feet long makes a rotor 16.4 feet in diameter, and the "swept area" is 211 square feet. The rotors on most turbines begin turning when the wind reaches about 7 miles per hour, although this can vary.[5]

WIND GENERATORS AND THE GRID

The small wind turbines for houses can be tied to the grid or not. States that offer rebates for wind power require a grid connection. Naturally, it costs much more to remain totally independent. In remote locales, though, staying off the grid is cheaper than extending the lines to the house. The California Energy Commission says that if the cost of extending electrical lines to the house costs more than $10,000, you should consider staying off the grid. On the grid, the wind power you collect runs your house until it exceeds what you need. When that happens, as it will on a very windy day or night, the power will automatically funnel out the lines to the street lines. The meter will run backward, and the power company will pay you for the electricity. In a storm, if the grid power cuts off, you have no backup energy stored at the house, even though you are hooked to the grid.

ONE COUPLE'S EXPERIENCE

In 2004, Becky and Phil Larson bought a house that came with a broken wind turbine in Elbert County, Colorado. "When Phil saw the turbine, he was just in awe," Becky Larson told reporter Steve Raabe of the *Denver Post*. She insisted that they weren't "radical conservation freaks," but admitted that the turbine interested her, too.

They decided to rebuild it. They spent $8,000 and reduced their $400 monthly electric bill to about $200. They heat with electricity.[6] At this rate they will earn back their investment in a little over three years, not to mention using clean energy for half of their power.

Facts About a Residential Wind Turbine in Colorado

If a house is remote or the monthly electric bill is more than $150 a month, a single residential turbine makes good sense, environmentally and financially.

Such a turbine costs between $35,000 and $45,000, including installation. It turns on an 80-foot-tall tower. The blades are 12 feet long, the rotor has a 24-foot diameter, and the swept area is 452 square feet. The peak output of this turbine is estimated at 10 kilowatts.

It will take about fifteen years or fewer to earn back the money in saved power bills.

SOURCE: *The Denver Post.*

The following chart compiled by wind consultant Mick Sagrillo shows the cost and output of several residential-sized wind turbine systems as of July 2005. Sagrillo says that many people are surprised to learn that the total cost—what he calls the "turnkey cost"—is considerably higher than the cost of the turbine and tower. This is because installation involves getting permits and erecting these very tall structures.

Sagrillo warns that the "rated output" in kilowatts "is a really poor measure of output of a turbine," because your own conditions affect its performance. Still, it's a guide to the size of a turbine.

The first five machines are cabin-sized machines designed for off-grid use. Of these tiny systems, only the Whisper 200 can be tied to the grid. The next six systems, from the Proven 2.5 through the XLS, are all small residential systems. The final three are big residential systems. These produce more power than my house would need.

You can calculate how long it would take to pay a system off by dividing the kilowatt-hour output (choosing ten miles per hour, or twelve) by what you now pay per kilowatt-hour. The figure will show you the amount of money you will save per month using your system. Multiply that number by twelve months for your yearly savings.

Then you must add in the cost of operation and maintenance. Sagrillo says to allow 1% of the total installed cost for a reasonable amount of money for yearly maintenance. Yearly maintenance always includes an inspection by the installer who will look for loose bolts and other problems.

For example, with the XLS, put aside $521 a year for operation and maintenance. The yearly inspection alone will probably cost less; Sagrillo estimates about $250. Put the rest in a bank account. After ten years of putting aside such funds, you should have enough for a set of blades or bearings.

The one exception to the rule of setting aside 1% of the cost for yearly maintenance is in the case of the Jacobs 3120. For this model, save 2%, because there are so many moving parts on this system.

Typical Prices for Installed Systems

Model	Swept Area, in square feet	"Rated output"	Turbine Cost	Tower	Typical Tower Cost	Turnkey Installed Cost	kWh/mo @ 10 mph	kWh/mo @ 12 mph
Lakota (by Aeromax, a Chinese company)	36.9	1 kW	$1,699	84'	$3,935	$14,700	96	155
Whisper 100	40	900 w	$2,085	84'	$3,935	$14,986	63	105
Bergey XL .1 (an American company, manufacturing in China)	58	1 kW	$2,450	80'	$1,890	$12,734	91	147
Cyclone (a Chinese turbine imported by Appalachian Wind Systems)	65	1 kW	$2,148	85'	$3,600	$15,137	163	260
Whisper 200	80	1 kW	$2,602	84'	$3,935	$14,981	124	193
Proven 2.5	97	2.5 kW	$13,665	105'	$7,364	$35,774	231	351
ARE 110 (made by Abundanta Renewable Energy)	110	2.5 kW	$8,700	105'	$4,400	$21,628	285	400
Jake Long	154	3.6 kW	$9,200	100'	$5,000	$28,063	350	520
Whisper 500	175	3 kW	$7,095	105'	$7,364	$31,079	341	538
Proven 6.0	254	6 kW	$22,439	120'	$10,850	$59,596	618	931

continued

Model	Swept Area, in square feet	"Rated output"	Turbine Cost	Tower	Typical Tower Cost	Turnkey Installed Cost	kWh/mo @ 10 mph	kWh/mo @ 12 mph
Bergey Windpower XL-S	398	10 kW	$24,750	120'	$10,850	$52,117	520	900
Jacobs 31-20 (made by Wind Turbine Industries Corp.)	754	20 kW	$21,255	120'	$14,887	$54,056	1,644	2,691
Vestas V-15-35	1,963	35 kW	included	110'	included	$105,000	3,354	5,371
Vestas V-15-65	1,963	65 kW	included	140'	included	$115,000	3,675	5,992

©2005 Mick Sagrillo

Wind Power: Fast Facts

Wind provided one-half of 1 percent of America's electricity as of 2005.

The American Wind Energy Association says it is realistic to expect that wind could produce 15 percent of America's electricity by 2030 or 2040.

The Netherlands generates 24 percent of electricity from wind power.

The wind in the United States could generate more electricity in 15 years than all of Saudi Arabia's oil.

One wind turbine can provide $2,000 to $4,000 per year in income on farms, while using between 2 and 5 percent of the land.

Wind turbines must stand very tall to work. The three-blade rotors must turn at *least* 30 feet *above* anything that would stand in the way of the wind—such as trees or ridges.

Manufacturers often tout the peak energy output of their turbines, relying on hypothetical conditions. When comparing products, consider the blade size. The longer the blades, the larger the "swept area," or amount of wind collected.

More than 2,000 megawatts of wind power, or enough to serve about 600,000 homes, were installed in the United States from 2003 to 2005.

The total installed wind capacity in the world, as of the end of 2004, was 47,317 megawatts or roughly enough power for 10 million households in the United States.

SOURCES: Wind consultant Mick Sagrillo; Reuters; the American Wind Energy Association.

CHAPTER FOUR

Other New Technologies: Hydrogen Fuel Cells, Biodiesel Fuel, and Geothermal Heat Pumps

HYDROGEN FUEL CELLS

The descriptions of the future "hydrogen economy" so far read a little like a science fiction novel. The U.S. Department of Energy asks the public to picture a world where hydrogen filling stations are on every corner, and where everything we can think of—from our cars to our laptops—potentially runs on hydrogen. Though this dream is not new, it has yet to come true. Researchers have described the hydrogen economy for at least three decades.

What they don't do is predict when that transforming time will arrive. Hydrogen fuel cells now power experimental cars and buses, and some institutions—including the Peabody Museum at Yale University—have begun to augment their heating systems with hydrogen fuel cells. Still, the full potential of fuel cells is far from being reached. The most promising of the hydrogen fuel cells emit water vapor, although it's still not clear whether this is as benign a byproduct as it seems. Researchers have warned of another byproduct of hydrogen fuel cells—the leakage of hydrogen. Researchers at California Institute of Technology have estimated that leaked hydrogen in a hydrogen economy could decrease the stratospheric zone [as cited by *The News Hour with Jim Lehrer*]. The other major problems are establishing a new infrastructure to service and "refuel" hydrogen cars and avoiding the use of fossil fuels, which so far are necessary to build the cells and to perfect the chemical reactions that create power in them.

Hydrogen, the most abundant element in the world, can be extracted out of other elements, such as water, natural gas, and coal. Researchers would like to find a way to remove hydrogen from biomass—that large category of burnable waste products that come from plant, wood, and even animal and human waste. Natural gas is the most common hydrogen source. The necessary electricity for extracting hydrogen can come from traditional fossil-fuel-burning power plants, or from wind turbines or solar photovoltaic cells that would link directly to the hydrogen production factory.[1]

In a fuel cell, two oppositely charged metal plates surround an electrolyte. Hydrogen and oxygen atoms enter from different sides. The hydrogen is split into protons and electrons. Protons continue through the *anode* (one of the metal plates) and electrons are directed through the circuit to generate electric power. The protons and electrons then meet on the other side, where they combine with oxygen that has been passed through the *cathode* (the other metal plate), and combine to form the cell's waste product: water. Both the heat and water by-products of this reaction can be captured and used for other purposes.[2]

While this technology sounds almost perfect—a dream come true for the environment—one major problem with it is providing the energy in the cell that performs the chemical reaction. For instance, two of the possible sources—or *feedstocks*—for hydrogen as a fuel are methane and water. In order to extract hydrogen from methane, you have to heat additional methane. In order to extract hydrogen from water, you have to provide electrical energy from a battery to begin a chain of events known as *electrolysis of water*. In electrolysis, water molecules break up into hydrogen bubbles and oxygen bubbles. The process of creating the hydrogen feedstock for fuel cells is not very efficient unless the hydrogen can be extracted without burning fossil fuels. If you must use fossil fuel to extract the hydrogen, the heating value of the hydrogen from the cell will be less than one-third of the heating value of the fuel burned in a power plant to extract the hydrogen.[3]

Hydrogen fuel cells for a house basement aren't on sale yet. Some companies and countries are working in earnest to make hydrogen the major fuel within thirty to forty years. Radian, Inc. of Alexandria, Virginia, and a Canadian company, Hydrogenics Corporation of Mississauga, Ontario, signed a contract in 2005 to manufacture a fuel-cell system for the U.S. Army Stryker light armored vehicle, known as an LAV. It would use a proton exchange membrane fuel cell and provide the hydrogen using electrolysis.[4] In Flint Michigan, Kettering University and the city's transit authority began work on a fifteen-passenger fuel-cell van and a forty-foot fuel-cell bus, which they hope to roll onto the Flint streets in the fall of 2006.[5] Iceland announced in 1999 that it would become the world's first hydrogen economy, and its leaders are working with major corporations such as Shell Hydrogen, DaimlerChrysler, and Norsk Hydro to convert Iceland's transportation sector to hydrogen over the next thirty to forty years, as Seth Dunn reported in a Worldwatch Institute paper in 2001. The first fuel-cell buses began driving in Iceland in 2002.

Dunn says that the impact of a move to hydrogen on the economy "will be staggering, putting the $2 trillion energy industry through its greatest tumult since the early days of Standard Oil and Rockefeller." Many companies are developing fuel cells to perform a huge range of tasks that would indeed make them as ubiquitous as electricity, if the plans come to be. Fuel cells would run cell phones and laptops, vending machines, houses and institutional buildings, cars, and planes.[6] Some companies are testing small fuel-cell systems that would generate from 3 to 10 kilowatts of power for houses. The expectation is that this electricity would be cheaper than what we can get today. Fuel cells have already been tried in hospitals and computer centers worldwide.[7] Micro fuel cells, to replace batteries, could someday power laptops, telephones, and portable generators.[8]

All but the skeptics—and there are some skeptics—believe that hydrogen fuel cells will mark a chapter in energy history as significant as the era when coal ruled, in the eighteenth and nineteenth centuries, or when oil took over, in the twentieth century. Worldwatch warns that the United States could lose its status as a superpower if it does not move to hydrogen technology soon. "Countries that focus their efforts on producing oil until the resource is gone will be left behind in the rush for tomorrow's prize," the Worldwatch authors wrote. "As Don Huberts, CEO of Shell Hydrogen, has noted: 'The Stone Age did not end because we ran out of stones, and the oil age will not end because we run out of oil.'"[9]

One of the most public of the skeptics, James Howard Kunstler, would not agree with these predictions. "The widely touted 'hydrogen economy' is a particularly cruel hoax," he writes in his 2005 book, *The Long Emergency*. "We are not going to replace the U.S. automobile and truck fleet with vehicles run on fuel cells. For one thing, the current generation of fuel cells is largely designed to run on hydrogen obtained from natural gas. The other way to get hydrogen in the quantities wished for would be electrolysis of water using power from hundreds of nuclear plants. Apart from the dim prospect of our building that many nuclear plants soon enough, there are also numerous severe problems with hydrogen's nature as an element that present forbidding obstacles to its use as a replacement for oil and gas, especially in storage and transport."[10]

For a professional coalition of fuel cell manufacturers, the World Fuel Cell Council, the conversion is happening too slowly. The council has said that the public does not fully support the new technology, so that costs are still high and few products have gone on the market. The council believes that city buses (tested since the 1990s) will provide the first major place for the new technology. "Hydrogen fuel-cell buses are now sufficiently technically advanced to enter the market, but extensive field demonstration and fleet testing is required to prove performance and build confidence in the technology," the council writes.[11]

Fuel-cell cars are also being tested. A Mercedes fuel-cell car tested in 1999 is twice as energy-efficient as a diesel version of the car—but the liquid hydrogen tank allows the car to go only 280 miles before refueling. Major car makers are aiming to sell hydrogen cars soon: DaimlerChrysler, GM, Ford, Toyota, Nissan, and Honda. Journalist Jim Motavalli test-drove a fuel-cell car in 2005 and reported that it worked quite well.[12] (For more, see chapter 7.)

Fuel Cells Are No Modern Phenomenon

The history of fuel cell studies shows even those of us who aren't scientists that the challenge has always been to devise a practical and inexpensive fuel cell. It all started in the nineteenth century.

A Welsh scientist named William Robert Grove developed a wet-cell battery in 1838. It generated about 12 amps of current. Scientists argued over still-developing chemical theories that would explain how current could flow in Grove's battery. In 1893, Friedrich Wilhelm Ostwald further explored the chemistry of Grove's fuel cell.

For many years, there emerged no practical applications of the fuel cell that would enable it to replace other fuels. European scientists continued to work on fuel cells. In 1889, Ludwig Mond and Carl Langer extracted hydrogen gas from coal and were able to generate 6 amps per square foot at .73 volts.

Meanwhile, two other scientists struggled with a similar fuel cell, complaining that gases leaked from one chamber to another. These two, Charles R. Alder Wright and C. Thompson, said that if the cost were no object, fuel cells could be built with large enough coated plates to allow enough current to be created. Others also believed that the cost was too high or that the savings to consumers were not high enough. William W. Jacques released his so-called carbon battery, which also used coal, in 1896. His battery turned out to be terribly inefficient, making power with a thermoelectric action.

Swiss scientist Emil Baur studied fuel cells in the early twentieth century using such materials as molten silver, clay, and metal oxides. O.K. Davtyan of the Soviet Union experimented with other materials.

Francis Thomas Bacon of Britain began studying electrolyte fuel cells in the late 1930s. He put aside his research during World War II. By the 1950s, he had developed expensive but relatively efficient fuel cells using potassium hydroxide instead of acid electrolytes. Pratt & Whitney licensed this technology for spacecraft.

A Canadian engineer, Geoffrey Ballard, developed a proton-exchange membrane in the 1980s. This created the chemical reaction necessary but at low temperatures. He began testing fuel cells in vehicles. In the 1990s, Daimler Benz (later DaimlerChrysler) developed a compact Mercedes that could go 280 miles on one tank of liquid hydrogen.

SOURCES: Smithsonian Institution (see its lengthy and helpful Web page on fuel cell history at http://americanhistory.si.edu/fuelcells and www.whyfiles.org.

BIODIESEL FUEL

The original diesel engine, invented by Rudolph Diesel in 1900, ran on peanut oil. Peanut oil and any vegetable oil can be refined to run automobile engines or furnaces. Since 1998, the federal government has counted biodiesel fuel as an alternative fuel, leading to an increase in the number of biodiesel users seeking a federal tax credit. The U.S. Postal Service and the U.S. Departments of Defense, Energy, and Agriculture use the fuel in their vehicles. The fuels are starting to run buses, vans, and garbage trucks.

The tax credit is one penny per percent of biodiesel in a fuel blend made from vegetable oils, and one-half penny per percent for recycled oils. This incentive is taken by petroleum distributors and passed on to consumers. The USDA has predicted that the demand for biodiesel will continue to rise. If petroleum prices continue to rise, biodiesel could become a bargain. Much of the biodiesel sold commercially today is made of soybean oil. It's available only in limited areas. It takes about 7.3 pounds of soybean oil, which costs about 20¢ per pound, to produce a gallon of biodiesel. Biodiesel costs at least $1.50 per gallon to produce. Used restaurant oils can produce fuel for as low as $1 per gallon.[13]

Some biodiesel users refine the fuel at home. Their experience illustrates the simplicity of the process. This chemical reaction can go on inside an old hot water heater perched in a garage or barn. The resulting fuel can either be mixed with Number 2 heating oil to make your heating furnace cleaner-burning, or used on its own in furnaces or vehicles. Biodiesel fuel reduces hydrocarbon and particulate emissions by more than half. If you use a mixture of 20% biodiesel and 80% fuel oil, you reduce emissions by up to 20%, according to *Mother Earth News*.[14]

How could people not have tried this sooner? Well, oil was so inexpensive until recently that most people wouldn't have bothered. Nevin E. Christensen, a Connecticut egg farmer and operator of a petting zoo, is now bothering. He has started making his own biodiesel in a shed. He uses the fuel to power his tractor. He starts with 200 liters of "old gunky waste veggie oil from restaurants," which he pumps into an abandoned eighty-five-gallon water tank. He heats the tank to 130 degrees. In a separate tub, he mixes ten gallons of methanol and three pounds of household lye (such as a product you'd use to unclog your drains). He pumps this by tube into the heated vegetable oil and mixes it for a half hour, then shuts it off. The glycerin settles out to the bottom. He removes it to run through old nylon stockings to make soap, the old-fashioned way. The remaining liquid in the tank is his tractor fuel.

"I never thought I could do something like this," he says. At first, he was scared when filling the tank. Vegetable fuel gives off no black puffs of particulates, as petroleum-based diesel does. The tailpipe smells like French fries. Vegetable-based biodiesel burns 75%

cleaner for all pollutants except nitrous oxides, he says. "We could grow 25 percent of our diesel fuel on land, now fallow, which the government paid us not to use."[15]

GEOTHERMAL HEAT PUMPS

The temperature six feet below the soil stays relatively constant, even in frigid climates, ranging from 50 degrees in the North to 70 degrees in the South. Geothermal heat systems circulate water or antifreeze through several hundred feet of pipes, called a loop, buried in the ground or submerged in a pond or lake. These tubes of fluid can serve either for heat gathering or heat dispensing, depending on the season. In winter, the system concentrates the earth's natural heat in the fluid and circulates it back into the house, and, then, using electrically driven compressors (sort of like an air-conditioner in reverse) and heat exchangers, it raises the fluid's temperature to 100 degrees or more, which can then be used to blow hot air through a house's duct system or can be pumped through a radiant floor heating system. Geothermal heat pumps generally cannot raise the water temperature high enough to be used directly in baseboard or radiator systems.

In summer, the heat pump works in reverse, drawing warm air out of the house. Systems can be rigged with a component that will loop into the hot water tank. This works best in the summer when there is extra heat to be had.

Two types of loop systems are used, depending on the size of the house's yard or property. Horizontal loops are used when the homeowner has a large-enough yard to bury hundreds of feet of tubing parallel to the surface of the ground. For small yards, a vertical system can be used, where pipes descend 150 to 450 feet into the ground.

Geothermal heat can be captured from the earth in either horizontal (opposite) or vertical (above) loops of pipe.

The only expense beyond the considerable equipment and installation costs is the electricity spent to circulate the fluid in the loops, and the electricity the heat pump compressor uses to bring the water temperature up to 100 degrees. Depending on pump size and house size, you can save 30% to 40% of the cost of conventional heating systems.

Heat pumps will cost you about $2,500 per "ton" of capacity, a commonly used measure. An average house uses a three-ton unit

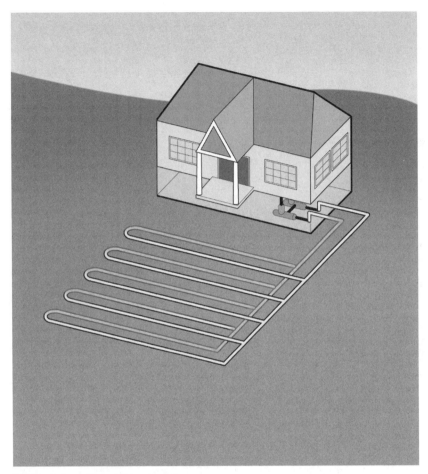

Horizontal geothermal heat system.

costing about $7,500. This is a bit more than the initial cost of a traditional heating and air-conditioning system, though, of course, the energy savings begin to mount from the time you buy your geothermal heat pump. If you finance the heat pump with a special loan (known as the energy-efficient mortgage), you might add about $30 per month to your mortgage payment. A good system will pay for itself in energy savings in between two and ten years, and the pumps last for twenty-five to fifty years.[15]

CHAPTER FIVE

Heating with Wood

In North America, people love heating with wood. But lately, there are reasons enough to feel guilty about it. We feel guilty using wood because fireplace fires draw heat out of the house while warming a tiny area. We feel bad because even though woodstoves heat efficiently, they—like fireplace fires—pollute the air. But woodstoves have been improved: the smoke coming from newer stoves is much cleaner than those made before the 1990s—as long as you maintain the stove. So none of these reasons should stop you from substituting some oil, natural gas, or electricity to heat part of your dwelling with wood. Yes, you must pay attention to the problems wood can cause if not burned properly or in the right kind of stove. That aside, many of the bad feelings that circulate about wood burning are, in my opinion, a useless exercise—on a par with feeling bad because we use any resources at all.

Woodstoves aren't the only home-heating method that pollutes. Almost every form of heating a house or apartment pollutes the air—especially because we're more inclined to crank up the heat with these systems than we are with a woodstove, which requires hand-feeding. Woodstoves may have gotten a worse reputation than oil-burning home furnaces, which are much more common.

Still, the pollution from woodstoves is real—and it can be worse if you neglect the stove. Government scientists have labeled woodstoves as major polluters because they emit microscopic burned matter known as *particulates*. This pollution includes polycyclic organic matter (POM), a large group of particulates formed from burning a long list of substances from steak on a grill to cigarettes to wood to automobile fuel. Seven of the POMs are classified as cancer-causing agents. Animals who inhaled one category of POMs in a lab setting developed tumors and leukemia.[1]

It is not difficult to understand why the government requires new woodstoves to filter out many of the particulates. The rules are part of "new source performance standards" of the U.S. Environmental Protection Agency. Manufacturers outfit new stoves with catalytic converters or after-burners, both of which ensure that particulates and carbon burn completely before the smoke goes up the chimney. These stoves won't continue to burn cleanly after the first few years if you don't clean them and keep the filtering components working. The catalytic converters have begun to fall out of favor because after several years you have to pay a few hundred dollars to install a new one. A new category of stoves have come on the market. These are known as *non-catalytic* stoves because the after-burners aren't catalytic converters. They aren't quite as clean-burning when new, but they remain fairly clean even when owners neglect them.

It seems a good bet that stove owners will get a little lazy with maintenance. When the EPA evaluated sixteen of the newer stoves in Oregon over forty-three weeks in the late 1990s, they found that cleaner stoves lost efficiency in filtering out particulates when they were only a few years old. Even so, "on average, after about seven years [the stoves] still have lower emissions than uncertified conventional stoves."[2]

It's within the power of an individual to burn wood cleanly in a newer stove that's properly cleaned and maintained. This is a better step toward improving air quality than unspecified guilt over large utilities' emissions. Older coal- and oil-burning power plants in America operate without having to upgrade to newer technology. So dare to enjoy a woodstove, which provides an affordable source of heat—especially if you can cut your own wood. And dare to feel proud that if you use a new stove, you're taking further steps than many power plants. Of course, we won't be arrested if we use older stoves. This is a voluntary program. Finally, feel glad that you are reducing the amount of oil, coal, electricity, or natural gas you would otherwise burn for heat in your house.

The reasons we love wood fires go deep into our backgrounds. It isn't just that we love to sit around crackling logs. It's because wood fires built America. Wood is a local fuel source for those who live in forested regions. It stands or lies ready on the ground (whether we gathered it up ourselves or not). It lights quickly and is easily put out. You control when the heat begins and when it ends.

Before 1900, 90% of Americans burned wood for heat, but as coal came into wide use, followed by oil, wood became unpopular except as an ambience producer. By 1970 only 1% of the population heated with wood.[3] After the energy crisis of the late 1970s, homeowners started burning wood again and there was a mini stove boom. In the 1980s, woodstoves fell out of favor because of the particulate pollution they emitted, and the federal government enacted stricter controls. This led to major improvements in stoves starting in 1985; woodstove manufacturers devised stoves that could cut the amount of nitrogen oxides, carbon monoxide, and particulates. Today's woodstoves burn cleaner than anything pre-1990.

Despite all this, burning wood does create particulate pollution, and anyone using wood for a fuel should do everything possible to reduce the pollution. The new stoves ensure that the least amount possible reaches the air. Woodstoves made after July 1, 1988, were required to meet pollution filtering standards set by the EPA. Two years later, in 1990, more stringent Phase II regulations went into effect. The new standards require new stoves with catalytic converters to emit less than 4.1 grams of particulate matter per hour. Stoves without catalytic converters must emit no more than 7.5 grams per hour.[4]

Critics say that even cleaner-burning stoves can't change the fact that wood still pollutes. That is true, but not in the sense that burning oil and coal pollutes. Those who champion wood for heat note that the carbon released during wood burning is the same amount that the wood would release if the tree were to fall to the ground and rot.[5] Coal, oil, and gas also release carbon when they burn, but these releases come from very old stores of energy that are burning now only because people have gone to the trouble to drill for them. Releasing that much carbon into the air over a few decades' time has altered our world.

Don't fall for the other famous argument (dating to President Reagan's famous, although not unique, comment that trees cause pollution), which asserts that trees and plants naturally pollute more than cars or factories. This is a skewed way of considering the fact that plants put more carbon dioxide into the atmosphere than fossil-fuel burning does. Yet plants are *supposed* to put carbon back into the atmosphere after they take it up. It is the burning of fossil fuels like oil and coal—which is *not* part of natural cycles—that have led to our current situation. Fossil-fuel burning alters the natural carbon cycle. People can't change the amount of carbon dioxide coming from trees. It will be the same whether burned in a stove or rotted on the forest floor. We can change greenhouse gas emissions by refraining from burning fossil fuels. These emissions would not exist without human beings.[6]

TWO WAYS TO HEAT WITH WOOD

One type of wood furnace is gaining popularity—**the outside wood furnace.** It offers both benefits and potential problems, according to Dirk Thomas, a chimney sweep in Vermont and author of *The Wood Burner's Companion.*[7] The benefits include that the wood fire burns away from your house, eliminating smoke, ashes, and inconvenience. Asthma and respiratory disease sufferers benefit. The down side is that many outside furnaces are quite large and can burn smokey fires. Many models are equipped with automatic shut-downs to prevent them from overheating the water in the boilers (which provide heat to the house).

If you live in the suburbs or city, where your neighbors are close, an outside wood furnace is not the best choice, because the chimney is low enough for smoke to be bothersome to neighbors. But in rural areas, they make a lot of sense. Be wise about the fire. Use dry wood, don't throw in trash or green stumps and, of course, maintain the unit. Finally, place the outside furnace where the prevailing winds won't bring the smoke into your house.

If your wood source is free you are hardy enough to split and feed the fire twice a day, installing an external wood burning unit is a good plan. If oil prices stay high, the furnaces can pay for themselves in about four years.

The hearth. For simplicity and ambience, not to mention flexibility, a woodstove provides an excellent source of heat, particularly as a backup to a furnace. If you spend most of your time in your house and don't mind tending a stove, you can provide most or all of a small house's heat as long as the stove is centrally located and the fire properly tended with good, dry wood.

BUY NEWER STOVES AND MAINTAIN THEM

In order to responsibly heat with wood, stove owners *must* take care of their stoves. Each year my fuel oil company calls and insists that we allow them to come to the house to clean the furnace. A woodstove owner must think in the same way. Call the chimney sweep each year. Check with the stove dealer on other routine work the stove needs. Be responsible and the stove will do the same.

Dan Melcon, a woodstove seller, said it's not fair that woodstoves have gotten a bad reputation since the late 1980s. Millions of old stoves are still out there, though, and he warned that people should

A Vermont Castings woodstove in action.

replace them soon. "The analogy I use is that it's as if people were continuing to use computers from the early 1980s," he said. Of course, many of those old stoves sit unused in the corner while people turn up the thermostat, as Melcon put it. So invest in a newer stove and take the old one to the metal pile for recycling. The air will benefit.[8]

IS THERE ENOUGH WOOD?

What if heating with wood were to take off in popularity and most people wanted to do it? Would Americans burn down all the surplus firewood in a few years? It seems highly unlikely. As attractive a method wood burning might be when considering the alternatives, using woodstoves will interest only those people willing to do a little work building fires, cutting, stacking, and carrying wood, and sweeping up ashes. For this population, there is more than enough wood. Forester Stephen Broderick of the University of Connecticut Cooperative Extension has studied wood supplies for burning for two decades and burns wood at his house. According to Broderick: "We grow significantly more wood in our forests each year than we cut, and the local forestry literature has for seventy years amounted to one long lament about the lack of markets for small, non-timber quality wood that needs to be thinned out of the forest in timber stand improvement cuts. We could demand several hundred thousand more cords of wood annually and still be fine if we had a system for assuring good forestry practice was employed in the harvesting."

By one estimate, a house that normally uses 500 gallons of Number 2 fuel oil in a year could produce the same heat using a wood furnace with 3.6 cords of wood. (A cord of wood is a wood pile 4 feet wide, 4 feet high, and 8 feet long, or 128 cubic feet.) A house that uses 60,000 cubic feet of natural gas per year would require 3.1 cords of wood to produce the same heat using an airtight woodstove.[9] This is much better than the twenty to thirty cords of wood used in fireplaces each season in Colonial New England.[10]

SCRAP WOOD, PAPER, AND WOOD PELLETS

It's not necessary to burn logs. My husband and I augment our heat supply with scrap wood from our town dump. (If you haven't done so already, seek out the trash-handling center closest to your home. If nothing else, it will provide a modern-day archaeological study of today's wasteful era. My casual estimate is that about half of what people throw away could still be used.) Small pieces of two-by-fours and untreated wood trim show up there every week. Because our woodstove is a secondary heat source, we have tried to make the wood supply as cheap as possible. Occasionally I've bartered with a friend for a trunkful of split logs. He gives me the logs from his hand-cut supply (from his own land) and I take a loaf or two of bread for his family. Not everyone has such easy-to-please friends who love chopping extra wood. Nevertheless, scrap wood is abundant. I see enterprising men in pickup trucks collecting the utility company's leavings from tree-trimming jobs. Construction debris may await you at the local lumberyard or renovating business.

Warning! When using scrap wood, be absolutely sure that it wasn't pressure treated. Identify pressure-treated wood—which is usually milled and cut for decks, lawn furniture, fences, docks, and other outdoor structures—by its greenish cast and smooth finish. It also has a distinct smell. Research studies have concluded that the common chemical used before 2004 to preserve such wood, chromated copper arsenate (CCA), seeps out of the wood into soil. When it burns, both the smoke and the ashes contain hazardous chemicals that could be absorbed through the skin or leach through soil to contaminate groundwater.[11]

BURNING WOOD EFFICIENTLY

The wood must be dry enough to burn efficiently. If you buy a cord or a half cord from a firewood cutter, you can be fairly sure the supply has seasoned, which means it sat drying for one year. But if you scavenge wood, be sure that any green wood sits for a season to dry out. Green wood doesn't look literally green, but some species do have a green tinge in the pulp. When you split a green log, the inside is supple. Green wood contains 40% to 70% moisture, says Ashford, Connecticut, wood expert John Bartok, a retired engineer from the University of Connecticut Cooperative Extension Center. Seasoned firewood is about 20% moisture. Burning green wood won't produce as much heat as burning seasoned wood. Burning green wood greatly diminishes the stove's efficiency. The stove can't get as hot, and creosote can build up in the inside, creating a fire hazard in the chimney.[12]

Another way to burn wood is to buy wood pellets made mostly of sawdust. Experts recommend that you don't burn these in regular woodstoves but use pellet stoves, which are designed to hold pellets. Pellets are easy to load and very dry—about 3% to 4% moisture—so they burn more efficiently than wood. Pound for pound, these cost roughly the same as wood. You can buy pellets through a woodstove dealer or home store.

The following chart illustrates something of a hypothetical situation—assuming that you can situate a woodstove centrally in a small house so that it provides all of the heat. The experts tell me this is very doable.

Most of us use woodstoves occasionally to provide some of the heat. I use this example to show the most you can get from your decision to burn wood if you are devoted to that as your heating method.

I assume that you are comparing the cost of a new woodstove to that of a furnace already in place. I assume that the cost of a cord of wood remains constant. Wood quality can affect how well it heats. Pine is less efficient than shagbark, the most efficient. I use white ash as an example because it's a middle-of-the-road wood that reflects a cord of mixed species.

When you consider costs, factor in chimney sweeping each year (about $75) and a maintenance cost of about $250 after the third year, either to replace the catalytic converter or to do other work.

Switching from Oil or Natural Gas to Wood Heat in a 1,500-Square-Foot House

	Stove cost	Wood needed/ season	Worst-case scenario	Best-case scenario	Oil furnace	Natural gas	Notes
Wood-stove, model 1	Encore, catalytic cast-iron, CFM $1,900 for basic model.	3.5 cords of decent hardwood	$250 a cord, total $900	You cut your own wood for free	700 gallons at $2.60/ gallon, total $1,820	About $1,700 in 2005	If you have free wood, the stove pays for itself in the second season. If you buy the wood, the stove pays for itself in in the third season.

	Stove cost	Wood needed/ season	Worst-case scenario	Best-case scenario	Oil furnace	Natural gas	Notes
Wood-stove, model 2	Dutchwest non-catalytic stove, cast iron. $1,349 (only in black).	3.5 cords	$900	Free	$1,820	$1,700	Whether you use your own wood or have to buy it, you recoup your money in the second season.
Wood-stove, model 3	Dutchwest steel non-catalytic. $1,079 (only in black).	3.5 cords	$900	Free	$1,829	$1,700	Whether you use your own wood or have to buy it, you recoup your money in the second season.

SOURCES: For woodstove models and prices, John Davidson, senior wood technical advisor, CFM Specialty Home Products, manufacturer of Vermont Castings stoves, Mississauga, Ontario. For cordwood prices, Dirk Thomas, a chimney sweep from Vermont and the author of *The Wood Burner's Companion*. For oil and natural gas prices, Energy Information Administration of the U.S. Department of Energy.

While all wood provides the same amount of energy per pound, the amount of wood per pound varies greatly from species to species. For instance, according to Iowa State University, a pound of basswood weighs 25 pounds per cubic foot, while shagbark hickory weighs 51 pounds per cubic foot.

The chart below, based upon data from the University of Missouri Extension, evaluates wood with a 20-percent moisture content. (It's crucial to aim for that percentage. Dry, or season, all cut wood for at least six months and preferably a year to eighteen months.) Wood this dry provides about 7,000 Btu's of energy per pound.

Heating efficiency also depends on the stove or furnace's efficiency and how well a house is insulated.

The heat output is measured in British thermal units (Btu's). One Btu is the amount of heat needed to heat a pound of water 1 degree F at its maximum density of 39.1 degrees.

Comparing Firewood Efficiency

Wood	Million Btu's per cord	Gallons of fuel oil needed to equal one cord	Tons of coal needed to equal cord	Cubic feet, in hundreds, of natural gas needed to equal cord	Gallons of propane needed to equal cord	Kilowatt hours of electricity needed to equal cord
Osage orange	30.7	219.3	1.28	307	337.4	9,029
Shagbark hickory	29.1	207.9	1.21	291	319.8	8,559
Black locust	28.1	200.7	1.17	281	308.8	8,265
White oak	27	193	1.1	270	297	7,941
Red oak	25.3	181	1	253	278	7,441
Sugar maple	25	179	1	250	275	7,353
Ash	23.6	169	1	236	259	6,941
Black walnut	21.8	156	1	218	240	6,412
Hackberry	21.6	154	0.9	216	237	6,353
Red elm	21.4	153	0.9	214	235	6,294

Wood	Million Btu's per cord	Gallons of fuel oil needed to equal one cord	Tons of coal needed to equal cord	Cubic feet, in hundreds, of natural gas needed to equal cord	Gallons of propane needed to equal cord	Kilowatt hours of electricity needed to equal cord
Sycamore	20.7	148	0.9	207	227	6,088
Elm	20.1	144	0.8	201	221	5,912
Shortleaf pine	19	136	0.8	190	209	5,588
Red cedar	18.9	135	0.8	189	208	5,559
Box elder	17.5	125	0.7	175	192	5,147
Cottonwood	16.1	115	0.7	161	177	4,735
Basswood	14.7	105	0.6	147	161	4,324

SOURCE FOR FIGURES: Publication G5450, University of Missouri Extension. See http://muextension.missouri.edu

CHAPTER SIX

Harnessing a Backyard Stream: Micro-Hydroelectric Systems

Making electricity with falling water is one of the most simple and fascinating concepts modern civilization has perfected. On a large scale, this requires giant dams to control the flow. But in someone's backyard stream, the dam can be quite small and the turbine is no larger than a car motor. Of course, you also need a backup method of providing electricity if a drought dries up the stream temporarily. For those who live near power lines, using a micro-hydro system might amount to a hobby, but perhaps not as expensive as building cars or flying around the world. The hardest part for anyone might be obtaining permits to install a micro-hydro system.

Using water for power goes back a long way. The first known dam was an earthen structure in Egypt 4,500 years ago. (The rains washed it away the first year.) In order to achieve a good flow without limiting all power generation to waterfall-side sites, civilizations going back to the Greeks 2,000 years ago wrestled the water into submission. Most of the time, that meant damming a stream or river so that the water flow could be controlled—and creating a lake behind it. At first it involved placing wheels in the water flow; the turning wheels turned other machinery. By the mid-1700s, scientists worked on new machines that could convert water flow into direct current (DC). By the late 1800s, the first hydroelectric power plant in the world went online in Wisconsin, producing alternating current (AC).[1]

Colonial America built itself on small-scale hydroelectric systems that powered mills and machinery. Hydroelectric power isn't benign: it interrupts rivers, changes fish migration, and even alters the rotation of the Earth ever so slightly because the artificial lakes weigh so much. But water replenishes itself and doesn't make air pollution. If hydroelectric plants include fish ladders, the damage to fish life isn't as great. Big dams continue to control water for power plants in the West and Northeast. The Hoover Dam across the Colorado River near Las Vegas, the Grand Coulee Dam across the Columbia River in Washington state, and the Shasta Dam across the Sacramento River in California all divert rivers into energy production for millions of customers. These dams are huge. Cars can drive across the top of the Hoover Dam, through which water travels at least 420 feet powering seventeen turbines and providing 2,080 megawatts of power. The Grand Coulee Dam, the largest concrete structure in the world, holds back Columbia River water to make Lake Roosevelt, which reaches from the dam to the Canadian border, 150 miles long. The Shasta Dam's spillway is 438 feet long, creating the tallest man-made waterfall in the world.[2]

In the 1990s, smaller dams—many left over from abandoned mills—began to be dismantled, along with warnings that dams threatened fish or waterways. We had barely gotten used to the modern ethic, most notable in the 1990s, of breaching or removing small dams on many of the lesser rivers across the United States, when the micro-hydroelectric movement started to re-gather steam. And so it's natural to wonder whether such systems hurt wildlife that lives in the flow of streams or changes the vegetation in them. Large reservoirs hold a lot of dead plants that encourage the kind of bacteria that will absorb mercury, which might be in the soil, leading to fish eating it. But in a micro-hydro system, the impounded water area is small.

ONE MAN'S SYSTEM

Richard G. Mackowiak lives in Eastford, Connecticut, on the tiny Still River, which joins the Natchaug River downstream. The hydroelectric plant in his yard dates to 1830. Mackowiak says that he set out to build, install, and maintain a new hydroelectric plant on his property that would power his entire house (including the heating system) and allow him to sell power back to the electric company. His intentions became a reality.

Mackowiak, his wife, and thirteen-year-old son live comfortably on the power, and he sells extra to Connecticut Light & Power. "On the average I make almost twice as much as I need, so in addition to supplying all my electricity, they do send me a small check once a month," he says. "I think I got a check for $34 or something. It's the energy portion of the electric bill."

In Connecticut, all of the various surcharges bring the kilowatt-hour price to more than 14¢ an hour (of which 5¢ to 6¢ is the energy itself). Mackowiak must pay that price like any customer, and he can sell his power back only at the wholesale rate, which is between 5¢ and 6¢ per kilowatt-hour. The result pleases him, even if he isn't making a lot of money. "We don't have any energy costs of any kind," he says. "There are no oil deliveries here. There is no gas line coming in off the street."

Mackowiak owned a business that sold hydroelectric equipment and recently sold out to a partner after twenty years. In other words, he intimately understands his equipment and knows how to take care of it—as you will need to if you want to try this. "I've done every-thing by myself," he says. "I'm the only one who knows the equip-ment in and out. I built it by myself, and I'm the only one who takes care of it. That puts me in a predicament. When I go on vacation, there's no one here to watch it. It's not like the furnace that you have down in your basement; you have the guy come down once a year and see if it's still there. You need to know a little bit about everything to keep it running. Mechanical, electrical, or carpentry repair."

He does not believe he'll live long enough to recoup his invest-ment. "Economically, I don't think anybody could justify it. But there are a lot of people like myself who do it because it's enjoyable."

The whole process took him so many years, and the cost is so tied up in his own time and labor, that he hasn't attempted to put a price on it. But he is glad he did it. "Whenever I tell the story as I'm telling it to you, I always have a smile on my face. It has been very neat. . . . [It] has taken a long time, but I think that's part of what makes it rewarding. Even building this project here in the backyard. It took me twelve years working on weekends to put the thing back together. To see it actually finished and working, it was just great."

HOW TO GET STARTED

Be certain your property contains the following features:

"Head" and "flow" in your waterway. The water in the stream or river must drop a distance before the water collects in a pipe to run a turbine. A waterfall is ideal, but most hydro systems, from the largest to the smallest, achieve *head* with an impoundment of water behind a dam. Systems can also work if established in the run of the river or stream, without an impoundment. The dam holds back water except a small amount that rushes through at high pressure. The stream or river must also contain enough water moving through at a fast-enough rate. The amount of water in the stream, which hydro contractors always call *flow*, is measured in gallons per minute. The higher the flow, the more power you can harness.

Ability to collect water at the highest point. The place where your micro-hydro system begins is at the highest point where you can set up the *intake*. Here is where the dam would hold back water and release it as pressurized head; or, perhaps, you have a waterfall and all you need is to place a screened pipe in it. It's important for the water to move quietly before it enters the intake pipe, since air or debris can damage the turbine below. The pipeline, or *penstock*, is the term for this quiet area of water.

Enough flow to provide 300 to 400 watts of continuous output. This will provide a household with all of the non-heating electricity it should need. (A basic rule of using alternative energy is to avoid using electricity to heat *anything*.)

In order to determine whether you can provide enough, your next step is to find a contractor. You need a turbine that is specially designed for your stream or river's conditions. Some turbines work immersed in water, while others sit mostly above the surface, activated when the flow hits.

To generate a supply of alternating current, you will need more water than if you install a system that stores direct current in batteries. (The battery system must connect to an inverter to convert the direct current to alternating current.) A contractor can help decide what sort of system you can install. For resources, see the Appendix.[3]

BE REALISTIC

Mackowiak makes it clear: a hydro system is expensive. Canadian micro-hydro dealer Paul Cunningham says that he actively discourages anyone

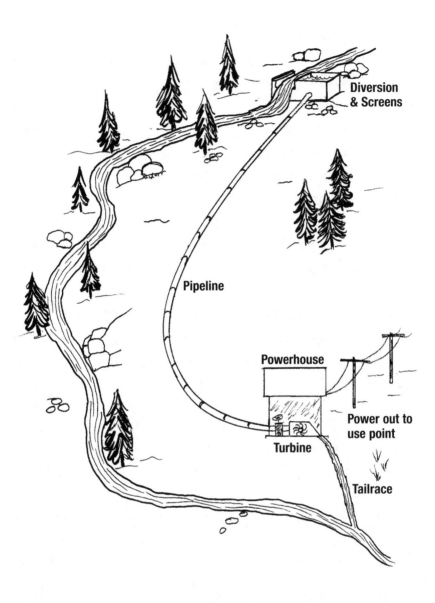

A small residential hydroelectric system includes a box that collects the water, called the *diversion*; the pipeline to create pressure; the turbine and generator; and a route for the water to flow back into the stream or river, which is called the *tailrace*.

Illustration by Dawn New, courtesy of Canyon Hydro of Deming, Washington who could otherwise hook into established electricity lines from trying hydro. But for those who live too far from electric lines to escape major costs of extending them to their property, an off-grid micro-hydro system could be cheaper than the cost of extending power lines.

Mackowiak says that you are best off using a dam that already crosses your stream. In New England, that is not that difficult. "Usually they were all built with this in mind, to produce power," he says. "All I've done in the back yard is to repair something that someone built 150 years ago."

Structures in streams usually require permits from several agencies. Mackowiak's permits came through in three years. There were no migrating fish that required a fish ladder, but "there were many fish concerns. When the FERC [Federal Energy Regulatory Commission] studies my application for a license, they involve all the people." They include the state environmental department, the U.S. Army Corps of Engineers, the U.S. Fish & Wildlife Service, and other agencies—all of whom offer observations and suggestions for operating the equipment without hurting the wildlife.

As a result of his permit requirements, Mackowiak is not allowed to use all of the water in the river. In dry summers, he has to turn off the turbine, sometimes for as long as two months. This ensures that enough water remains in the river for the fish.

All this means that you need some sort of a backup generator. In Mackowiak's case, he's hooked to the power grid, so whenever he isn't producing power, he's buying it. The flow of electricity to the house is never interrupted.

THE REALITIES OF THE GRID

Hydro systems are specialized enough and expensive enough that most people who use them do not connect to the grid. "Ninety-nine percent of our customers are off-grid," says Cunningham, a partner in Energy Systems and Design of Sussex, New Brunswick, Canada. He says that it's not even worth your while to try to compare the costs of staying connected to the power grid with getting your power from your stream or river. "If you try to make it look good, it won't," he says. It's too expensive. Also, you have to figure in that power from the grid is generally heavily subsidized. Figuring the environmental costs if we continue burning fossil fuels for most electricity is also quite complicated.

"The playing field is nowhere [near] level," Cunningham says. "Every day I have a conversation with somebody who thinks they are going to save money or make money. I say, you're not going to buy anything from me."

He's so tough with his words because he wants potential hydro owners to understand the commitment they'd make and the cost. He has little patience for the question of comparing utility-supplied electricity's cost to the cost of using a hydroelectric system. "Once people use the payback [question], I almost slam down the phone," he says.

Cunningham also says that if you do use an alternative technology like hydro, and if you do not connect to the grid, you will naturally use less power. "If you have utility power, you tend to overuse and use rivers of energy and think you're using a trickle," he says. "Almost invariably the people who call me up and want to do this, they don't want to use less power. They want to switch seamlessly from one type of power to another."

He says, "The point I will make again and again is: If you can reduce your needs . . . why would you invest in anything? First thing I said was: over ninety-nine percent of our customers are off-grid. That's our customer base. The people who are on-grid, as soon as I find out they have commercial power, I try to do away with them, in a gentle way."

CHAPTER SEVEN

Alternative Cars

As petroleum begins its slow decline and the world population continues to increase, drivers will have to catch up to the changing reality slowly. I'm the last person to scold anybody. I drive a lot myself (I'm a devoted car recycler; right now I drive a 1995 Mazda 626 given to me by a friend). But all of us must face it. Our driving habits and the efficiency of our cars need some upgrades. Cars and trucks burn 27% of all the energy burned in America. Thirty years ago, vehicles burned 25% of the total burned. Besides this, the rate of increase in energy use for transportation sped up in the 1990s.[1]

The efficiency of the American vehicle fleet today is worse than it was during the energy crisis of the 1970s. As a whole, the fleet averages 20 to 21 miles per gallon. The Model T Ford was more efficient than that. Plus, half of our vehicles today are cars and trucks. "That's not progress," says Jeff Deyette, an energy analyst with the Union of Concerned Scientists in Boston.[2]

The whole thing is rather embarrassing. If you've decided to fight this, the fight is a little easier than it was a few years ago. It's easier to buy an alternative vehicle today than it was only a few years ago, but the demand is greater than the supply: it's typical to have to get on a waiting list for a gas-electric hybrid car. Until the mid-2000s, the automobile industry had delayed mass-producing alternative vehicles and even spent some effort arguing against their use. The first hybrid vehicle wasn't available in the United States until 1999, when the Honda Insight first went on sale here. The next year, the Toyota Prius began selling in America.

Other experiments went awry. When GMC recalled an electric pickup truck issued in limited quantities in California, electric car lovers demonstrated. The zero emissions were nice, but the trucks did not save fuel because they relied on fossil fuel for the battery that runs it.

Other alternative vehicles began to take off in numbers and popularity in the United States in 2005. Gas-electric hybrids have finally landed in the ordinary American's consciousness, although the numbers being produced are still small. Hybrids use gasoline to power a

If the option exists, the best gas-saving step you can take is riding your bike to work.

battery system that allows the engine to switch periodically to straight battery power, saving a lot of fuel.

Toyota aims to sell only 100,000 Prius models in 2006, for example. There are now eight hybrids on the market, with more to come. In May 2005, Toyota Motor Corporation announced it would produce a gas-electric hybrid Camry in late 2006 at its Georgetown, Kentucky, plant. So far all hybrids have been made overseas. Toyota said it would be able to produce 48,000 of the new hybrids each year in Kentucky.

HYDROGEN FUEL-CELL CARS

In May 2005, the U.S. House of Representatives passed the Clean Cars 2 initiative (HB 6908) to develop financial incentives for those who buy energy-efficient cars. In June, the Connecticut State Assembly passed a bill to set up financial incentives for clean cars, the first such bill of its kind in the country.[3]

That same month, May 2005, Honda lent its FCX, an experimental hydrogen fuel-cell car, to journalist Jim Motavalli, who drove it for 265 miles over the space of a week, interrupted only by the car's trip in a trailer to a refueling station in upstate New York. Motavalli reported he was pleasantly surprised at the car's speed and efficiency—almost like a gas-powered car. The FCX (Fuel Cell Experimental) can only go about 190 miles before refueling, and, so far, it's possible the cars would only last about 30,000 miles (not to mention that the country would need a network of hydrogen refueling stations). Why this has taken so long is a good question. At former president Jimmy Carter's inauguration in 1977, a hydrogen Cadillac was on display. Now, three decades later, the experts and the government predict that it would take another decade or two of research before the public could buy and use hydrogen cars.[4] For more on how hydrogen fuel cells work, see chapter 4.

HOW HYBRID CARS WORK

Hybrids run on both a gasoline engine and an electric motor. Brutally simplified, the gasoline engine runs the car and also charges the electric motor, which kicks in under certain conditions. When a driver stops a car, say, to wait for someone in a driveway or at a stop sign, the engine turns off completely, bringing on an eerie quiet. As the car research Web publication Edmonds.com explains it, hybrids fall into two categories. Some hybrids run on only the electric motor at low speeds, and therefore get better mileage in city driving conditions; examples are the Toyota Prius and the Ford Escape Hybrid. But other hybrids are no better than a traditional car in city driving conditions, because the electric motor kicks in only to boost the gasoline engine when accelerating or going uphill. This second group of hybrids includes the Honda Insight and the Civic Hybrid.

The Edmonds.com Web editors explain that, "a Toyota Prius accelerates from a standstill, the electric motor gets the vehicle rolling and continues to drive it up to around 25 mph before the gasoline engine automatically starts up. Under hard acceleration from a stop, the gas engine starts immediately to provide maximum power. . . . Because the electric motor is used so much at low speeds, the Prius and Escape get better mileage in the city than they do on the highway."

But the Honda hybrid models use the electric motor only when the car needs a boost—"such as during hard acceleration from a stop, while climbing a hill, or passing other vehicles. As with normal, gas-powered cars, these hybrids get better fuel economy while cruising on the highway, as that is when the gas engine is least taxed."

Although the electric motor runs off battery power, the hybrid technology automatically recharges itself through normal braking and coasting action. Here is how this works. The Ford Escape, Honda Insight, Honda Civic, and Toyota Prius all use sealed nickel metal hydride batteries, or NiMH batteries, like the batteries that power cell phones and laptop computers. The number of individual battery cells varies from car to car. The Prius batteries rate nearly 274 volts. The Honda hybrids provide 144 volts. The Ford Escape Hybrid, 330 volts. As the car coasts on a downgrade, or when the driver puts the brakes on, the system reverses its polarity, and the electric motor automatically becomes a generator, converting the movement and braking into mechanical energy that the batteries store.[5]

The public isn't quite ready for this

The car makers aren't making as many hybrid cars as those who want them. But they believe the general public isn't quite ready for this. Toyota sold about 54,000 hybrid cars in 2004, according to Toyota Motor Sales spokesman Bill Kwong, and production was about that number. "The waiting list was anywhere from eight months to one year. Basically we sold everything we made." In 2005 they planned to manufacture and sell 100,000 Prius models. If there is a waiting list, why not make a lot of these cars? Kwong insists it's not time yet. Toyota is manufacturing more than six times as many Corollas, compared to Priuses. Camrys are even more abundant, with almost 426,000 manufactured in 2004.

"Prius is actually our third best-selling car," Kwong says. As of 2005, it was still manufactured solely in Japan, while the majority of the number-one and -two best-sellers, Camrys and Corollas, are made in North America.

With the Prius, "we have a goal—to sell every one," Kwong says. "Some might carry over into the following year. We have a sell-down. We have a push." Worldwide, Toyota hoped to sell 300,000 Priuses in 2005, with an eye for selling half a million by about 2015. Nevertheless, he says, hybrids are still an alternative, but not what mainstream America wants. He says that it's for "someone who wants the latest and greatest, who wants to be environmentally friendly."

Most car buyers don't look at environmental factors, according to researchers at the University of Maine. In 2004 a group of professors and students interviewed Maine residents about their attitudes on car buying. The motivation was to evaluate car makers' publicity about energy efficiency. Maine was devising a sticker that could go on new cars proclaiming the efficient ones "green." The study results showed that people have a lot to learn, still. Here's a quote from the study results:

The moderator then asked participants whether they ever thought of environmental issues when shopping for a car or truck. Participants generally did not consider environmental impacts when shopping for a vehicle. When the moderator asked why they did not take these issues into consideration, many stated that they felt that air emissions were not a problem with vehicles; they said that vehicle emissions were already heavily regulated and that the regulations basically made all cars "pollute about the same."[6]

I called Jonathan Rubin, a professor of resource economics and policy at the University of Maine, who directed the study. He said, "People don't recognize that there's a difference between cars. They don't realize that cars have different environmental footprints. They think that the government is taking care of that."

He said people don't connect the way they live with their choice of car. "They think—curb appeal. And they don't think, 'Is this the environmental statement I want to make?' "

It used to be a great truth of the auto industry that people who buy hybrid cars were die-hard conservationists, a decided minority. That's not true anymore. Drivers who wouldn't have touched a hybrid a few years ago have gotten on the waiting lists to buy them.

When you buy a hybrid, yes, you want to reduce the number-one cause of global warming, auto exhaust. But this chart shows that hybrids can also be a money-saving choice. The higher gas prices climb, the better the deal.

My chart—while it uses an arbitrary set of conditions—clarifies that some hybrids pay for themselves quickly, while others do not. Most of the mid-sized hybrids pay for themselves if you tend to drive a car for several years before replacing it, or if the price of gasoline is high. For most larger hybrids, the payback is only environmental, and extremely slight, at that.

The hybrid trucks barely save any gasoline. In order not to lose engine power, the engines use a milder hybrid, or "mybrid," technology that results in less efficiency than other hybrids offer. (You have to ask yourself if it's worth it at all to buy a hybrid truck. Wouldn't it be better to cut out one trip a week?)

I have compared major hybrid models on sale in late 2005 to similar non-hybrid cars, using hypothetical parameters. I did not take into account car repairs and maintenance. These are base models without extra features. I have averaged city and highway miles-per-gallon estimates from a number of sources.[7] My mileage figure assumes you'd drive about equal amounts on the highway and in town.

For comparison, I chose non-hybrid cars very similar to the hybrids in size, engine size, and convenience, but these are *not* identical. The Honda Insight has no non-hybrid counterpart, so I compared it to Honda's most efficient non-hybrid, the Civic.

I worked with base prices without added features. I picked a middle-of-the-road yearly mileage figure. I picked a gasoline price projected for 2006 by the U.S. Energy Information Administration. If you don't drive much, it will take you longer to recoup any car investment. On the other hand, you are doing the right thing not to drive much.

Finally, I make no claims that this is scientific. Fluctuating gas prices, differing driving habits, and inflation, will alter the results. If you'd like, get out a calculator and play around with your own figures.

How Long It Takes to Make Back Your Hybrid Car Investment

Hybrid Model	Base price	City mpg	Highway mpg	Average mpg	Yearly gas bill if driving 30,000 miles and if gas costs $2.40 gallon	Comparable non-hybrid car, price, average mpg, and yearly gas bill	Approximate length of time to recoup the extra cost of the hybrid, if gas costs $2.40 gallon
Ford Escape Hybrid	$26,350	36	31	34	$2,118	Ford Escape V6 $21,015 20.5 mpg $3,512 yearly gas bill	Under 4 years (Pay $5,335 more for hybrid) (Save $1,394 a year in gas)

Hybrid Model	Base price	City mpg	Highway mpg	Average mpg	Yearly gas bill if driving 30,000 miles and if gas costs $2.40 gallon	Comparable non-hybrid car, price, average mpg, and yearly gas bill	Approximate length of time to recoup the extra cost of the hybrid, if gas costs $2.40 gallon
Toyota Prius	$20,975	60	51	55	$1,309	Toyota Camry 4-cylinder automatic $20,125 29 mpg $2,482 yearly gas bill	Under a year (Pay $850 more for hybrid) (Save $1,173 a year in gas)
Toyota Highlander Hybrid Midsize SUV	$33,030	32	27	30	$2,400	Toyota Highlander 6-cylinder 2-wheel drive automatic $26,190 22 mpg $3,273 yearly gas bill	Under 8 years (Pay $6,840 more for hybrid) (Save $873 a year in gas)
Honda Insight Hybrid Compact Coupe/ hatchback	$19,330	60	66	63	$1,143	Honda Civic manual transmission $13,260 35 mpg $2,057 yearly gas bill	6 and a half years (Pay $6,070 more for hybrid) (Save $914 a year in gas)
Honda Accord Hybrid	$29,990	30	37	34	$2,118	Honda Accord Sedan $16,295 30 mpg $2,400 yearly gas bill	48 and a half years (Pay $13,695 more for hybrid) (Save $282 a year in gas)
Honda Civic Hybrid	$19,900	46	51	49	$1,469	Honda Civic manual transmission $13,260 35 mpg $2,057 yearly gas bill	11 Years (Pay $6,640 more for hybrid) (Save $588 a year in gas)

continued

103

Hybrid Model	Base price	City mpg	Highway mpg	Average mpg	Yearly gas bill if driving 30,000 miles and if gas costs $2.40 gallon	Comparable non-hybrid car, price, average mpg, and yearly gas bill	Approximate length of time to recoup the extra cost of the hybrid, if gas costs $2.40 gallon
Lexus RX 400h Midsize SUV	$48,535	31	27	29	$2,483	Lexus RX 330 4-wheel drive $36,025 22 mpg $3,272 yearly gas bill	Nearly 16 years (Pay $12,510 more for hybrid) (Save $789 a year in gas)
Chevrolet Silverado Hybrid Pickup Truck	$30,345	18	21	20	$3,600	Chevrolet 1500 Pickup Truck $19,040 19 mpg $3,789 yearly gas bill	60 years (Pay $11,305 more for hybrid) (Save $189 a year in gas)
GMC Sierra 1500 Hybrid Pickup Truck	$31,770	18	21	20	$3,600	GMC Sierra 1500 Truck $19,040 19 mpg $3,789 yearly gas bill	67 years (Pay $12,730 more for hybrid) (Save $189 a year in gas)

SOURCES: Individual car manufacturers; Wired magazine (April 2005); www.fuel economy.gov; www.carprices.com.

Delivery Services Experiment with Hybrids

Federal Express and the United Parcel Service have begun using alternative trucks with what looks like success—but it has unfolded very slowly.

In 2004, Fed Ex and Environmental Defense introduced eighteen "OptiFleet" medium-duty Fed Ex delivery trucks in Sacramento. The company announced that these trucks, designed by the Eaton Corporation, would increase fuel efficiency by 50 percent and cut particulate emissions by at least 90 percent. The Sacramento Metropolitan Air Quality Management District helped pay for them.

By mid-2005, Fed Ex had rolled out no more hybrids but promised that it would add as many as 75 more by mid-2006, "contingent upon pricing and availability." The company said that it hoped the hybrid would eventually replace every one of its 30,000 medium-duty delivery trucks.

UPS began exploring new technologies a few decades back. Its "green fleet" includes more than 1,000 compressed natural gas vehicles, more than 3,000 low-emission diesel trucks, and eleven liquefied natural gas tractor-trailers. UPS is experimenting with hybrid and fully electric vehicles, and is testing fuel-cell trucks in Michigan. These alternative trucks are only a small fraction of its roughly 70,000 delivery trucks.

The federal government originally funded the compressed natural gas trucks but no longer does. (Here is a reminder why companies don't jump completely into the waters of new technology. They have to make money.)

Business Week magazine reported in 2003 that experts expected hybrids to be the best of all the options for efficient delivery trucks. They require little maintenance, the brakes last longer than traditional brakes (because the engine helps slow the car), and, of course, hybrids use less fuel. Fed Ex expected to break even on its first hybrid vehicles in about a decade.

One consultant estimated that more than 500,000 hybrid vehicles would be in service by 2008 and that 40 percent of these would be trucks. Let's hope.

SOURCES: Releases from Federal Express and United Parcel Service; Charles Haddad, "Fed Ex and Brown Are Going Green," *Business Week* magazine, August 11, 2003.

The more you begin to study the hybrids the more obvious it is that choosing one is part of a comparison game. Some of them don't save a great deal of gas. Until the world switches over to some technology that doesn't burn petroleum, the only way to reduce emissions is to save gas. Consider the obvious point—that you don't have to buy a hybrid to save gas. It is better to drive a car like the Volkswagen Golf, Volkswagen Jetta, or Volkswagen New Beetle (38 mpg in the city; 46 mpg on the highway) than any hybrid that uses more gas. These three cars ranked third on the list of the most efficient cars in 2005, compiled by the online car magazine Edmonds.com.[7] (The first two on that list were the Toyota Prius and the Honda Civic Hybrid.) A regular Honda Civic was the fourth-most efficient car on that list. Heck, even a Pontiac Vibe (it came in eighth) saves more gas than most of the hybrids manufactured now. It gets 36 mpg on the highway.

This leads to another obvious point, but one I still struggle to remember: If we don't drive at all, we don't use gas at all.

Photovoltaic panels provide electricity for this house in Gardner, Massachusetts.When the people who live here don't need the power, it flows out to the power grid. PHOTO BY BILL EAGER, NATIONAL RENEWABLE ENERGY LAB

Jimmy Carter's solar panels on a Unity College roof. COURTESY OF UNITY COLLEGE

Homeowners in mountainous Peshastin, Washington, make power from the wind with this Bergey Excel turbine, designed to generate 10 kilowatts under optimum conditions. It stands on a 100-foot-tall tower and is tied to the power grid. PHOTO BY ABIGAIL KRICH, NATIONAL RENEWABLE ENERGY LAB

A tiny wind turbine on the roof peak collects energy that will power the lights at Galehead Hut in the White Mountains of New Hampshire. AUTHOR PHOTO

Photosimulation of the Cape Wind project from six miles away. Cape Wind is a 130 turbine offshore wind farm proposed off the coast of Cape Cod, Massachusetts. The developer estimates that the project would produce as much power as 113 million gallons of oil and it would power three-quarters of the Cape and Islands energy needs. PHOTO COURTESY OF CAPE WIND ASSOCIATES

Blades from a wind turbine with other turbines in the distance. AUTHOR PHOTO

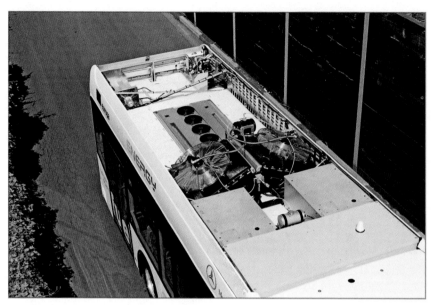

The fuel cell that powers this Mercedes-Benz Citaro city bus is located in the roof of the bus. PHOTO COURTESY OF DAIMLERCHRYSLER

In this cutaway view of a car's fuel cell, hydrogen and oxygen react to produce water, creating electrical energy. PHOTO COURTESY OF DAIMLERCHRYSLER

The United States Department of Agriculture has produced a soy-based fuel at its Agricultural Research Service's research center in Wyndmoor, Pennsylavnia. Here, electrician Alvin Coates fills the tank of an aerial hydraulic lift bucket with the experimental biodiesel. Biodiesel made from soybeans costs less to produce than some other plant-based fuels. PHOTO BY KEITH WELLER OF THE USDA

A look under the hood of a Toyota Prius. Because most gasoline engines are more powerful than usually necessary, a hybrid-electric car has room for a small gasoline engine and an electric motor. The electric motor is powered by a battery which is fueled by the gasoline engine. Electronic controls make the car's various engines work together. PHOTO COURTESY OF TOYOTA MOTOR SALES U.S.A

This micro-hydroelectric plant in King Cove, Alaska, serves a community of 700 people in an area so remote that residents were paying 21 cents per kilowatt hour for diesel fuel-generated power. This plant is a larger version of what homeowners in more remote areas can use for a few people. This plant diverts moving water from two creeks 250 feet downhill, generating 800 kilowatts of electricity. PHOTO BY DUANE HIPPE, NATIONAL RENEWABLE ENERGY LAB

This small hydroelectric turbine converts moving water to electricity with a hidden belt on wheel, similar to the one propped on the outside. PHOTO COURTESY OF CANYON INDUSTRIES, INC.

Outdoor wood-burning furnaces, or boilers, can heat an entire house, along with hot water systems, swimming pools and more. They're best used in a rural setting, where the smoke won't bother neighbors. AQUA-THERM WOOD FURNACE (OR BOILER) INSTALLED BY PETE MOSTEHRT OF DELHI, NEW YORK.

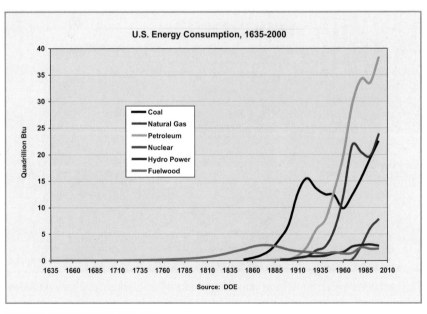

COURTESY OF WORLDWATCH INSTITUTE

CHAPTER EIGHT

Conservation: Not a New Idea

The most obvious tactic to reduce energy usage—using less—has never caught on for very long in the United States. When policy makers and power companies predict future electricity supplies, for example, have you ever noticed how they talk about meeting customers' *demand*? They might recommend that people conserve electricity, but mainly they consider the challenges of meeting whatever demand the people present. What exactly is demand? That word encompasses their best guess at all of the electricity people need and want. It covers necessities like heat, cooking, industry, and essential trips. Demand also covers the nonessentials like appliances and lights left on when no one is using them, unnecessary road trips, televisions blaring to no one, heating and cooling systems left on high for absent owners, etc. When utilities brace for brownouts in the summer and discuss meeting demand, perhaps they show more respect for us average Americans than we deserve. Some of our power uses are necessary, and some of them aren't. Our failure to distinguish between needs and wants does not put all of our power demands in the same category as a hospital's needs. Demand is a label that shields us from our own shortcomings.

In the last century or so, when Americans have conserved energy, we have done so out of dire necessity—such as during the Great Depression, World War II, or the energy crisis of the 1970s. The population *has* managed to save energy during crises like war or when oil prices spike. When each crisis ends, though, so does conservation.

A crisis can lead to savings, and from time to time, government leaders carry the flag for conservation with impressive results. In 2001, Californians achieved the great feat of reducing their electricity usage by 11% to avoid the threat of losing power. In the spring of 2005, Japan's government began a unique publicity campaign to inspire its citizens to use less electricity. It asked Japanese white-collar workers to stop wearing suits in the summer so that the air-conditioning could be set to a warmer temperature. To push the new dress code, Japan's environment ministry promoted a casual uniform it called Cool Biz. The look included cotton shirts and conservative pants, but no jackets. "The government will take the lead in prevention of global warming," Prime Minister Junichiro Koizumi was quoted as saying in *The New York Times*. "From this summer, government is planning to start no necktie, no jacket." Japanese men shunned an earlier casual business campaign in the 1970s, when the government pushed a suit with cut-off sleeves.[1]

Perhaps conservation is so difficult in everyday American life because we don't see ourselves as we truly are. We don't see how our decisions about where to live and how to live use up energy. Consider the exurban development explosion in places like Colorado, where houses are going up on large lots scattered across a wide expanse of previously open countryside. In Colorado, 144,000 acres of farmland each year over the last four decades has disappeared under other kinds of uses.[2] Similar statistics greet you in most other regions of the United States. The energy toll this kind of development takes on our resources became clear in the 2000 Census. The average commute to work from the exurbs, the outer ring about 50 miles from Denver, was thirty-eight minutes, the Census reported, compared to twenty-four to twenty-six minutes from closer-in suburbs and in Denver. "A commuter who drives 50 miles to work—25,000 miles a year—pumps out enough carbon dioxide, a key greenhouse gas, to fill a Goodyear blimp."[3] In many towns in northeastern Connecticut, the last largely rural region from Washington to Boston, housing developments are cropping up at a fast rate. The increases in long-distance commuting between 1990 and 2000 in northeastern Connecticut were higher than the national average. The intrepid workers were commuting by car to as far away as Boston and New York.[4]

We're losing our untrammeled land at great cost to the environment. Not only is animal habitat being reduced, but we're using more energy to live, scattered on large plots of land across the regions. The people who buy houses in the former backcountry love nature, I'm betting, which is why they want to live out in it. Many of the homeowners I have read about in the last few years are young to middle-aged professional adults who telecommute part of the week and relish their part-time semi-rural lives, away from the hubbub. They spend hours and lots of gas getting to and from their refuges. They are starting to turn around and realize that they aren't the only people doing this, discovering they are not intrepid individualists but part of a trend. It is easier to waste energy and resources in this way of life—especially if these people treat their outposts as if they were suburbs by making frequent trips into town.

If they are true to their ideals, assuming they moved to the exurbs because they value the land, they'd avoid daily car trips to the places from which they fled. Or they'd find another method of travel. But they can't; not today. The trolley lines of the early twentieth century no longer exist. Trains are rare, too. So there is a responsibility that goes along with the decision to move far away from services, and the responsibility includes the need to save energy—to live more truly like a hermit, not just to do so for a few hours at a time.

Saving energy happens in how you live. It happens within the walls of your house or apartment. In the last few decades, manufacturers have designed energy-efficient appliances that save a great deal of power over the appliances they replaced. The most dramatic improvements are in the new refrigerators and washing machines, two of the largest energy eaters at home. Improved house-building techniques trap heat indoors in the winter and cool air in the summer.

In other ways, we've made little progress conserving energy. During one of the crises many people alive today recall, the energy crisis of the mid-1970s, two engineers suggested that the best ways to cut home energy use would be, first, to insulate houses; second, to buy more efficient air conditioners; and third, to take buses or trains. Looking at these three recommendations in 2006, it seems that they remain good suggestions. That is, we still need to follow them.

First, consider the advice to insulate houses. The U.S. Department of Energy reports that homeowners pay for, and send outside, as much energy through badly insulated doors and windows as the Alaskan pipeline can deliver each year.[5]

Next, consider air conditioners. We should still try to reduce the power they use, but doing this is challenging because air-conditioning has taken over the indoor world since the 1970s. Efficient air conditioners alone can't reduce power when the number of buildings that use air-conditioning outweigh those that do not.

The energy crisis engineers' third idea, to take the bus or train, has remained only a hope in those places that weren't already relying on public transportation. The car still rules suburban, exurban, and rural America. Our public transportation system is limited to the very large cities. It was the best in the world in 1900, when trolley lines extended for great distances into backwater places. In 1923, the number of streetcar riders in America was 15.7 billion. By 1929, it had dropped to 14.4 billion, and by 1940, to 8.3 billion. Cars and buses took the place of the torn-out trolley lines. The passenger railroads crashed somewhat later, in the 1950s, when the government subsidies went to the air and automobile routes, bankrupting the railroads over the next twenty-five years or so.

"Unlike European governments, Washington treated public transportation as if it were a private business, while regarding the motorcar as worthy of immense public subsidies," wrote Kenneth T. Jackson, Columbia University historian and author. "Indeed, Senator Gaylord Nelson of Wisconsin reported that between 1945 and 1980, 75% of government expenditures on transport went for highways, and only 1% went to public buses, trolleys, or subways. The inevitable result of the bias in American policy, a bias that began even before the Interstate Highway Act of 1956 and one that has no counterpart in either Europe or Asia, was that by 1991 the United States had the world's best road system and very nearly its worst public transit offerings."[6]

In order to follow the advice to use the car less, we'd have to change our lives. But we can't leave the car at home if we live in one of the many, many places where it's our only means (aside from walking or bicycling, that is) to get to work or school. If work or school is more than a mile or two from home, that demands a sort of sacrifice that people shouldn't have to make. But we can begin to examine the number of unnecessary trips we make in our cars. In the days of more common public transportation and fewer cars per household, people didn't make a few trips in a day of ten, twenty, or fifty miles—just to find a good sale or visit a new store. They did errands closer to home. Today in most places it's just so easy to jump in the car. Our way of life, our expectations of endless energy, still drive our deepest behavior.

At the same time, we have started going farther to do things that enhance our lives, and if we have to give these up, life would go backward. My daughters, for instance, go to school, visit friends, volunteer, and take lessons in far-flung towns, requiring drives of twenty to forty miles round trip. They take a bus to school, but we drive them everywhere else. Thirty years ago, we probably wouldn't have taken them that far. Perhaps we should be working harder to consolidate trips and activities so we drive less.

Expecting endless energy supplies might be a modern trait, but it comes from the incredible plenty around us. When problems pinch the energy supplies, we still have the ability to conserve energy, because humans have always done that. Energy conservation originated in the beginning of recorded time. People of long ago conserved energy for fear the supply would run out, while they conducted their lives only to provide what was enough—and no more. But in today's world of science and exploration, where growth is considered good, this attitude doesn't prevail. Going back to before 1300, as former environmental policy maker Lindsey Grant writes, people did not believe that economic growth was a natural force. "Then came the Renaissance, which led to the Age of Exploration to the new world and new wealth," he wrote. "It started the agricultural and industrial revolutions and set in motion a worldwide scientific enterprise that is still accelerating. . . . That period has lasted, with minor interruptions, for six centuries. . . . It is a formidable belief system, but its proponents have forgotten that its origins were not in population growth, but in the Black Death, the most widespread and severe population collapse in human history." It left survivors with more farmland and more wealth.[7]

The term *energy conservation* dates only to the environmental movement of the 1970s. In earlier industrial times, it was called *energy efficiency*, and it referred only to how well appliances, industrial components, and systems operated. Of course, people used less energy if the supply was dwindling. On the frontier of America, pioneers conserved coal because it was so expensive to ship. In the 1970s, Americans conserved energy only because of the Arab oil embargo. For those who grew up in that time, energy conservation presented itself as something we would not have to practice forever. It was supply based. The sooner environmentalists today accept this connection, the better the chance that we can make conservation part of the nation's energy policy, which so far it is not.

It would be nice to believe that the environmental movement that took off in about 1969 and lasted through the late 1970s was the result of our realization that we were hurting the planet. Some of it was just economics, though. In 1975, the Congressional Research Service compiled a series of documents about energy conservation. The readings included presentations before Congress on conservation; articles from David B. Large's book *Hidden Waste: Potential for Energy Conservation,* which the Conservation Foundation published in 1973; journal articles on power generation; energy use on farms; and reports on energy policy proposals.

In the introduction to the collection, an unnamed author writing for the collection's producer, the U.S. Senate's Committee on Interior and Insular Affairs, wrote: "In the past, it was less costly to waste fuel than to use it efficiently. However, now, as a result of higher fuel costs, fuel scarcity, and our national dependency on foreign sources, energy conservation has been recognized as a national imperative."

Up to that time, energy policies were built on encouraging "industry to meet whatever demand is created in the marketplace." And that would have to change. (These words sound as if someone could have said them around the time oil prices began to shoot up in 2004.)

One of the articles reprinted in the congressional collection first appeared in the journal *Science* in 1974. Hans H. Landsberg wrote that the oil and natural gas shortages had changed the way people were thinking. "The United States has entered an era of profound alteration in traditional patterns and trends in the field of energy," he wrote. "Although the Arab oil embargo of recent months has greatly aggravated the crisis, the underlying causes lie farther back in the past and hopes of long-term remedies lie well into the future." He said the trouble had begun a few years before, when natural gas suppliers stopped hooking up new customers, when heating oil shortages closed some schools and public buildings, when Midwestern farmers worried about getting enough fuel, and when gas stations began shortening hours. Abroad, the Organization of Petroleum Exporting Countries (OPEC) revised contracts to deny access to supplies and "drastic, unilateral price boosts, with grave economic and political ramifications."[8]

Clearly, the mood in the mid-1970s was one of crisis, and I sense between the lines of the congressional energy readings that the country was up to gathering its courage to get through it. Gary Althen says in his book *American Ways,* "Americans cling to these values: individualism, equality, informality, progress, speed, and assertiveness. Not on the list are frugality and conservation. Still, it's the American way to cope through hard times, and that mentality could change how we use electricity, gasoline, and other energies."[9]

You might think that today you are ready to step outside the American mainstream. You want to save energy because waste makes no sense, ethically. And I agree with you. But this kind of altruism has little track record in modern America, and everywhere you look, you find a sober truth emerging. Conservation is barely a micro-trend. Humans, particularly modern American humans, don't seem inclined to link every small act of comfort at home to the burning of fuel or every small act of sacrifice to the greater good of the community. There seems to be one reliable way human beings in any country can be made to conserve energy, and that is if the supply is limited or cut off. Here are the ways this could play out:

- We would have to use less energy because it would be against the law to use above a certain amount. This seems unlikely just on the merit of a law, unless something actually happened to the fuel supplies. The next scenario is more likely.

- We would have to conserve because energy supplies from distant sources are wobbly. We would start producing our own power, at home. Therefore, we wouldn't want to work harder than necessary to provide for ourselves, so we would naturally conserve energy, out of that innate trait of self-interest.

Paul Cunningham, who produces micro-hydroelectric systems in Canada for people who live away from power lines, believes most people don't realize how little power they need to live. "If you were using the minimal amount of power—lights, refrigeration, washing machine—that only takes about $20 a month worth of power." The rest, he says, goes into waste or into the various appliances that heat things (like hot water heaters, dryers, and irons). Anything that heats uses a tremendous amount of power.

"If there's 720 hours in a typical month, we get 216 kilowatt hours per month. If you are paying 10¢ a kilowatt hour, that's $21.60.

If you're using more than that, then you have room to improve," says Cunningham.

Cunningham adds that to run a household with four people using standard appliances, as he's outlined above, requires 300 watts of continuous power. Asked if we Americans are living like spoiled brats using too much energy because subsidies make it cheap, he says yes.

He makes the sensible case that if you choose to live off the power grid, you will necessarily waste less. "If you have unlimited power, you probably will leave the lights on, and you will buy things that use more power," he says.[10]

Looking back on the occasional emergencies or experiments when people managed to change their ways clarifies how easy it is to cut back on energy use. With ordinary restraint, the American public can redefine what the utilities and government love to call our energy "demand."

Consider the California rolling blackouts of 2001. The state predicted rolling blackouts due to a lack of electricity for the expected demand, so a huge campaign unfolded to get the state through the summer. Organizations handed out compact fluorescent bulbs. The power use did go down. Comparing two almost identical days, weather-wise, in 2000 and 2001, the statewide power use was 44,906 megawatts on August 2, 2000, versus 40,384 megawatts on August 17, 2001. Seventy-nine percent of a surveyed group reported that they had cut their energy use in some way.

Then consider this bizarre experiment in saving hot water in a college athletic field house in 1982 and 1983. Researchers set out to test the power of suggestion on the length of hot showers in the locker room. First they posted signs in the bathrooms that said, "Short showers save energy." As a result, 6% of the students took shorter showers. When a larger sign replaced the first, 19% cut back their showers, but people complained about the annoying reminder sign. When the researchers planted a student volunteer in the showers—with the instructions to turn off the water while soaping up whenever someone else was showering in an adjacent stall—49% of students did the same. The percentage increased to 67% when two volunteers, instead of one, enacted the water-saving measures.[11]

The college bathroom study proved that nudging people's consciences, even with a slightly annoying sign, can make people more responsible. It also proved that good behavior rubs off on others, leading to a higher level of responsible behavior. With that in mind, try the conservation tips listed in the next chapter—assuming you don't perceive the list as an annoying written reminder—and then watch while other people you know follow your example.

Most important, learn to think of the need to save energy as our response to a crisis that much of our world hasn't yet accepted. What many of the experts have been trying to tell us these last few years is that our definition of normal is going to change, even if there's no sign of it yet. Chauncey Starr (a physicist who pioneered study in nuclear reactors and president emeritus of the Electric Power Research Institute), said it well in 1973, and his words still speak to the way we "demand" energy: "The 'crisis' designation tends to be misleading," he wrote, "because it implies that quick-fix emergency steps should be taken to cure situations which have developed over many years. In fact, there are no quick fixes. Further, the practical realities of the situation have not yet required an immediate national 'crisis' response by applying true emergency measures—such as energy rationing and cessation of energy-consuming activities."[12]

CHAPTER NINE

Conservation Tips

These suggestions assume that you want to stay where you live right now and have no plans to build a new house. Most of these suggestions address people's behavior and the appliances they choose. These are actions that work in any sort of dwelling.

TURN OFF IDLE COMPUTERS

In general, the less time a PC is turned on, the longer it will last, and the more energy you save.

A computer uses the same amount of energy to turn on as it does to operate for about two seconds. It does not hurt a computer to turn it off ten or more times a day. The computer will wear out or become outdated before any wear and tear from that would affect it.

Plug the computer into a power strip and whenever you will not be using the computer for extended periods, turn it off using the switch on the power strip. If you use the buttons on the computer and leave it plugged in, it will continue to draw some power. If you have no power strip, unplug the computer when you aren't using it.

If you are not going to be on the computer for more than about twenty minutes, turn off the monitor. If the break is two hours or more, turn off the central processing unit (CPU) and the monitor. If you tend to go away and come back to the computer frequently during the day, turn off the monitor when you leave the desk. But if you aren't using it for four hours or more—and this counts for going to bed at night—turn off everything.

The only time you would leave the computer on is if you have a very old computer, if the computer operates a phone, facsimile, printer, or security system, or if the computer is part of a network.

SOURCE: U.S. Department of Energy, Energy Efficiency and Renewable Energy Web site, www.eere.energy.gov/consumerinfo/factsheets/ef3.html.

HEAT AND COOL LESS

Recognize that heating and cooling systems use the most power in the house—up to half.

To get used to using less energy for heat, turn the thermostat lower in tiny increments over a period of a few weeks.

When going away on vacation in all but the coldest months, turn heating or cooling systems completely off. To do this requires going to the unit and following instructions from the manual. Even in the summer, many furnaces remain turned on.

SOURCE: *Slash Your Energy Bills*, by Allen Lawrence. San Antonio, Texas: Ambient Environmental Concerns, 1977.

EVALUATE APPLIANCES— UPGRADE TO CONSERVE

To figure watts when the appliance lists amps, multiply the number of amps by the number of volts provided through your wiring (usually 110 volts). Amps times voltage equals watts.

The electric stove: In his book *The Natural House,* Daniel D. Chiras advises people who are building new houses to install propane stoves. "The large burners on an electric stove use about 1,200 watts of power when on high. The smaller burners consume about 600 watts of power." Propane may not be ideal—because it's fossil fuel—but it's much cheaper than electric to use and the emissions are minimal.

The microwave oven: Energy experts will tell you that a microwave uses about half of the energy of a conventional oven— but beware. This is true only as long as you are not using the microwave in a wasteful way. *The Consumer Guide to Home Energy Savings* estimates that a microwave can bake a casserole more efficiently than any other oven. See the chart. But, on the downside, people use microwaves for tasks better done on the stove, such as boiling a cup of water for tea, or using no heat at all, such as defrosting frozen food, which can be done in the refrigerator with a little forethought.

SOURCE: Alex Wilson, Jennifer Thorne, and John Merrill, *Consumer Guide to Home Energy Savings* (Washington, D.C.: American Council for an Energy Efficient Economy, 2003).

The following table from *The Consumer Guide to Home Energy Savings* compares the cost of cooking a casserole in several ways. It assumes the cost of gas is $.60 a therm, and electricity is $.08 a kWh.

Cost of Cooking

Appliance	Temperature	Time	Energy	Cost
Electric Oven	350	1 hour	2.0 kWh	$.16
Electric Convection Oven	325	45 minutes	1.39 kWh	$.11
Gas Oven	350	1 hour	.112 therm	$.07
Electric Frying Pan	420	1 hour	.9 KWh	$.07
Toaster Oven	425	50 minutes	.95 kWh	$.08
Electric Crockpot	200	7 hours	.7 kWh	$.06
Microwave Oven	"High"	15 minutes	.36 kWh	$.03

The refrigerator: Refrigerators use a good deal of a home's energy, and Americans seem to want more of them as time passes. The Worldwatch Institute reports that the average size of American refrigerators increased by 10% from 1972 to 2001. And yet many refrigerators use much less energy today than they did. The cost to run a typical new refrigerator (with automatic defrost and a freezer on top) is about $55 a year. In 1973, the typical refrigerator cost about $160 a year to run.

SOURCES: The Worldwatch Institute, http://www.worldwatch.org/pubs/goodstuff; Unitil (Fitchburg, Massachusetts), www.services.unitil.com.

By law, all refrigerators carry a bright yellow tag labeled "Energy-Guide." It explains how much electricity in kilowatt-hours a refrigerator uses. Refrigerators the federal government certified as low-energy always carry a tag labeled "Energy Star."

The following chart shows only a handful of the hundreds of models certified by the government as low-energy.

Refrigerators: Low-Energy Models

Refrigerator model	Kilowatt-hours per year (Energy Star estimate)
Abscold ARD1031F10RL Top freezer, 10.3 cubic feet	331
Amana ASD232411E Side-by-side 22.6 cubic feet	580
Crosley CRTE187E Top freezer, 18.3 cubic feet	407
Frigidaire CRTE187A Top freezer, 18.4 cubic feet	407
General Electric DTH18ZBS Top freezer, 18 cubic feet	410
Kenmore 318410C Top freezer, 18.4 cubic feet	407
Sub Zero 611 Bottom freezer, 16.6 cubic feet	465
Sun Frost RF-16 Top freezer, 14.3 cubic feet	254

DISCARD THE OLD CLOTHES WASHER

Dozens of clothes washers available today at reasonable cost save from one-third to three times the energy your old one uses. The main feature to look for is a front-loading, tumble design that uses much less water (and therefore less heat).

The following chart shows a fraction of the energy-saving clothes washers certified by the U.S. government through its Energy Star program. For more information, see www.energystar.gov. The Web site includes a calculator tool to figure your savings. You can plug in details particular to your area such as electricity rate and how many loads you do each year.

Energy-Saving Clothes Washers

Washer	Kilowatt-hours/year (Energy Star estimate)	Percent better (than the minimum Federal Standard)
Whirlpool LHWO-050	212	168%
Speed Queen CT599	224	82%
Miehle W1203	127	96%
Maytag Neptune MAH5500B	273	67%
Kenmore 4415	219	92%
GE WSXH208A	250	58%
Asko W6461	127	140%

INSULATE THE HOUSE

Do it yourself or hire someone to do it.

Replace or improve windows, where a lot of heat leaks. Put up storm windows earlier in the season than before, and leave them up longer. Change to thermal glass and use thermal drapes.

If you live in the right climate, plant deciduous trees near the house. In the winter, they'll let the sun through. In summer, they'll cool the house.

Insulation comes in several materials and thicknesses, each right for a specific area of a building and climate. The federal government has established a rating system for insulation, measuring its ability to resist the flow of heat (that is, its ability to hold heat inside). The higher the R-value, the thicker the insulation, but it's important not to use the wrong thickness. Insulation for the foundation and floors differs from that used on walls and ceilings. Insulation best in California wouldn't work in Tennessee.

It's not necessary to use commercial insulation, but you will have to do more work to learn how to use sheep's wool, straw, mixtures of straw and clay, cotton and plastic, and hemp—all of which can hold heat efficiently.

SOURCES: Fact sheets and publications by the Oak Ridge National Laboratory, www.ornl.gov. I recommend you peruse this Web site.

Daniel D. Chiras, *The Natural House: A Complete Guide to Healthy, Energy-Efficient, Environmental Homes*. White River Junction, Vermont: Chelsea Green Publishing Company), pp. 370–372.

A Consumer's Guide to Energy Efficiency on the Web site of the U.S. Department of Energy's Energy Efficiency and Renewable Energy program. See www.eere.energy .gov/consumer.

IMPROVE THE FURNACE

It's unavoidable to expend some sort of energy to heat the house at least part of the year in most of North America. Even if you use a woodstove (see chapter 5), you probably will need, at the very least, a backup furnace using natural gas or Number 2 heating oil. The U.S. Environmental Protection Agency requires furnaces to divert a minimum of 78% of the fuel it burns to heating the house. (The remainder goes up the chimney.) Old furnaces can do much worse than this—about 65%—while the best of the new models are 97% efficient.[1] You'll recoup your investment and help the environment. Maintain your furnace with annual cleanings to keep it running efficiently.

SOURCE: Consumer Search, www.consumersearch.com, furnace ratings.

TURN OFF THE TELEVISION

A thirty-six-inch television uses 133 watts of power. If it's turned on for twelve hours a day, 6 days a week for 313 days a year (allowing for when you're away from home), it will cost you $42.50 a year to run (at 8.5¢ a kilowatt-hour).

But if you leave it on only six hours a day, the cost becomes $21.23 a year. Just two hours a day costs $7.07 a year. Okay, this doesn't sound like much, but the amount does add up with other conservation measures.

SOURCE: Fact sheets on energy efficiency from U.S. Department of Energy, Energy Efficiency and Renewable Energy, http://www.eere.energy.gov/consumerinfo/fact sheets/ec7.html.

TURN OFF LIGHTS, SWITCH LIGHTBULBS

According to the Worldwatch Institute, lights use up to 34% of the electricity generated in the United States. Compact fluorescent bulbs use one-third to one-fourth the electricity and last ten times as long as incandescents. They can be used in standard bulb sockets. The Worldwatch Institute says that if every household replaced the most-often used incandescent bulbs with the compact fluorescents, the amount of electricity powering lights would be reduced by half.

Compact fluorescents produce the same amount of light (measured in *lumens*, one lumen equaling one candle's light) but they also don't cast that acid-like greenish hue they once did. My family experimented with compact fluorescents in the basement and in our reading lamp in the living room, and the difference is negligible. They cast a warm light with no discernible flicker. We will be switching most of our bulbs this year.

Start small: The Union of Concerned Scientists recommends that you start the switchover by replacing the five most-used bulbs in the house with compact fluorescents. The pinch of buying them won't feel as bad, and you'll hopefully be able to see a discernible change in your electric bill. For an estimate of the sort of savings for each bulb, see the chart below.

Warning: Don't throw used fluorescent bulbs in the regular trash. They contain mercury, a poison that can get into the food chain and continue to accumulate there.

SOURCE: The Worldwatch Institute's online guide to conservation at home, "Good Stuff." See www.worldwatch.org/pubs/goodstuff. Also, author's interview with Jeff Deyette, energy analyst, the Union of Concerned Scientists in Boston.

Incandescent Versus Compact Fluorescent Bulbs

Bulb type	100-watt incandescent	23-watt compact fluorescent
Purchase price	$ 0.75	$11.00
Life of the bulb	750 hours	10,000 hours
Number of hours burned per day	4 hours	4 hours
Number of bulbs needed	About 6 over 3 years	1 over 6.8 years
Total cost of bulbs	$ 4.50	$11.00
Lumens produced	1,690	1,500
Total cost of electricity (8¢/kilowatt-hour)	$35.04	$ 8.06
Your total cost over three years	$39.54	$19.06
Total savings over three years with the compact fluorescent:		$20.50
Total saving over six years		$52.00

This chart, compiled by the U.S. Department of Energy's Energy Information Administration, is also available for viewing on a Web site of the California Energy Commission, www.consumerenergycenter.org.

HOT WATER HEATER

The U.S. Department of Energy estimates that water heating accounts for 20% or more of an average household's annual energy expenditure. The yearly operating cost of a gas water heater is about $200, and of an electric, about $450. Conserving hot water can be the single most important conservation step you take. Change the heater to a solar-powered one (see chapter 2). Limit shower lengths and install a low-flow shower head, available from hardware stores and through some water companies. Buy a front-loading washing machine (see the section on clothes washers). Avoid rinsing dishes when loading a dishwasher; these machines are designed to handle some food on the dishes.

SOURCE: U.S. Department of Energy, Energy Efficiency and Renewable Energy on-line fact sheet, http://www.eere.energy.gov/consumerinfo/factsheets/bc1.html.

WASH DISHES CAREFULLY

Should you wash dishes by hand or with a dishwasher? It depends on how you handle either. It's possible to waste hot water whether washing by hand or using a dishwasher.

If washing by hand, here are some tips: Don't run the hot water every time you have a few dishes, and don't rakishly swipe with the sponge on things and try to simultaneously rinse. Washing by hand can save water, but only if you consolidate dishes and wash many at one time. I learned this technique from my mother-in-law, who serves meals for twenty in a cottage: Fill a tub with sudsy water, wash everything in proper sequence to maximize the suds (start with silverware and then dishes that touched people's mouths; proceed next to bowls and plates, then serving dishes, and, finally, pots). Then, rinse everything at once. Some people rinse in a clean tub of water, going in the same sequence as for washing. Others run the water over each item, turning it off in between rinses. That can be tedious, but it provides a cleaner rinse.

If you aren't up to this, a low-energy dishwasher (so rated by the U.S. government's Energy Star labels) is the best choice. Run it on a short cycle. Don't wash the dishes twice by over-rinsing before load-ing. Don't use the heated drying cycle. Open the door and let the dishes air-dry. If you have turned down your water heater to 120 de-grees to save energy, as we have, but worry about sterilizing the dishes, as we have, many dishwashers offer an "energy boost" button. It uses more energy, but only for the dishes.

SOURCE: My years of hard-earned wisdom in the kitchen, and also *A Consumer's Guide to Energy Efficiency* on the Web site of the U.S. Department of Energy's Energy Efficiency and Renewable Energy program. See www.eere.energy.gov/consumer.

A BATH OR A SHOWER?

Because showers and baths account for about a quarter of a household's water use, this is an area where we must cut back. Short showers use less water than baths. Beware the trap of daydreaming in the shower, solving all of your problems as you create more for yourself, allowing excess hot water to run down the drain. Consider the following:

- Bathtub capacities: 30 to 75 gallons.

- Older shower heads use 3.5 gallons per minute.

- Low-flow shower heads use 2.5 gallons per minute or less.

Use this data to calculate the best way to save water. It's pretty clear that unless you like baths in a few inches of water, showers usually will save energy. Just divide the number of gallons in a bath by the number of gallons per minute your shower head uses, and your answer will show how many minutes you would have to shower to fill the tub that high.

For instance, let's compare a low-flow shower head to a modest 30-gallon bath. As long as you take a shower that is shorter than 12 minutes, you will save water in the shower. No one should be taking a shower this long.

SOURCE: Water Resources Research Center, College of Agriculture, University of Arizona, *Water in the Tucson Area: Seeking Sustainability*. See www.ag.arizona.edu.

Surveying Energy Use at Home

Electricity

Gather electric bills for the past year. Utilities can provide copies of bills, or printouts of several months' use, on request. Record the kilowatt hours (recorded as "kWh" on bills) your house or apartment used on a month-by-month basis. Then add the total for the year.

month	kWh
Total kWh =	

To learn the impact of each resident of your house, divide your total kWh figure by the number of residents.

Per capita electricity use = _____ kWh.

continued

Next, you must calculate how much fuel your utility burned to provide your electricity. The figures in the calculations below were devised by Peter Markow, a professor at St. Joseph's College in West Hartford, Connecticut, based upon actual data from power sources in the northeastern United States.

Nuclear power plant:

Consumes .0005 uranium fuel pellets per kWh.

To determine how many uranium fuel pellets are needed for your house, multiply 0.44 x your total kWh x .0005:

0.44 x _____ kWh x 0.0005 pellets/kWh

0.44 x _____ x 0.0005 = _____ uranium fuel pellets

Oil-burning power plant:

Burns .066 gallons per kWh.

To determine how many gallons of # 6 fuel oil are needed for your house, multiply 0.29 x your total kWh x 0.066:

0.29 x _____ kWh x 0.066 = _____ gallons # 6 fuel oil

Coal-burning power plant:

Burns .78 pounds of coal per kWh.

To determine how many pounds of coal are needed for your house, multiply 0.05 x your total kWh x 0.78:

0.05 x _____ kWh x 0.78 = _____ pounds of coal

Trash-to-energy plant:

Burns 3.5 pounds of trash per kWh.

To determine how many pounds of garbage must be burned to provide electricity for your house, multiply 0.08 x your total kWh x 3.5:

0.08 x _____ kWh x 3.5 = _____ pounds of garbage

Heat

Home Heating Oil

Find your home heating bills for the past year and determine the number of gallons used at your house. Divide by the number of people in your house to determine your annual use of home heating oil.

date	gallons	date	gallons

Total gallons = _____

gallons/person = _____

Liquefied Propane or Natural Gas

Find your home gas bills for the past year and determine the number of pounds, cubic meters, or other unit of measure recorded on them. Divide the total used by the number of residents in your house or apartment to determine your annual use of natural gas.

date	lbs or cubic meters	date	lbs or cubic meters

Total lbs or cubic meters = _____

lbs or cubic meters/person = _____

continued

Car Gasoline

To figure how much gasoline you burned driving, determine the total number of miles you have driven your car in the past year.

Then divide the total miles driven by your average miles per gallon for your car.

_____ miles driven in the last year divided by _____ mpg (your car's average) = _____ gallons you burned.

SOURCE: Peter Markow, Saint Joseph College, West Hartford, Connecticut

CHAPTER TEN

An Appliance Manifesto

There is a specter haunting North America, and it just might be the fleet of electric appliances crowding our houses and apartments. Which appliance is bad and extraneous? That is a difficult question. For one family it might be the free-standing freezer, sucking up about one-eighth of one family's electric bill while they forget about the heaps of frozen meat hidden within. Or it might be the clothes dryer, running too hot and too long, costing hundreds of dollars a year. Whatever it may be, I now present my manifesto for each citizen to get rid of several appliances. While I suggest a list here, I can't force you to choose these particular gadgets. Perhaps you'll be inspired to find others. The only criterion is that they use electricity to perform tasks that could be handled without electricity.

In 1964, I was five years old. My parents took me and my three brothers to the World's Fair in New York. The General Electric (GE) home show so captivated me that I refused to leave the auditorium to go to the ladies' room. My parents liked to repeat this story of their little daughter who would let nothing stop her from watching the entire home show with its life-sized dioramas of the American kitchen from the 1890s through the 1960s. Walt Disney himself created this show. Each period kitchen took up a segment of a circular stage. The audience revolved around the stage several degrees for each act, depicting a new era roughly twenty years later than the previous one. Mechanized mannequins chatted about their appliances and lights as they looked out at the audience. All of the kitchens seemed homey, although each looked sleeker than the last.

When the home show moved to Disneyland as "Progressland" a few years after the World's Fair, it added a final act set in the near future—meaning in the late 1960s—in which a family ambled through an indoor mall near a nuclear power plant. The mannequins in this new scene discussed the wonders of inexpensive and clean energy. Here is a snippet of dialogue from that last act:

> *Mother: "Today our whole downtown is completely enclosed. Whatever the weather is outside, it's always dry and comfortable inside."*
>
> *Father: "General Electric calls it a climate-controlled environment. But Mother calls it . . ."*
>
> *Mother: "A sparkling jewel. Now far off to your right, we have a welcome neighbor . . ."*
>
> *Father: "Our GE nuclear power plant, dear."*[1]

To my parents and their peers, progress in this postmodern world, after World War II, meant that everyday life no longer involved heavy labor. Everyone, even a five-year-old girl, could understand the comforts and promise in new technology. I think of the early 1960s as one of the most hopeful times in modern American history. Home appliances had wrought a sea change in home routines. Jet travel and space exploration were becoming everyday events. But traditional social mores had not yet begun to unravel. In this era, sometimes called the postmodern, people placed an uncomplicated faith in the new comforts. There was a feeling that our parents deserved them after the hard years of the Depression and World War II.

A lot has happened since then. The Vietnam War, the hippie time (including the back-to-the-land movement), the disco era, the energy crisis, the "Reagan Revolution," the first Iraq war, the dot-com boom, the global warming controversy, the events of September 11, 2001, the second war in Iraq. . . . Today might well be called the post-post-modern era. The optimism of the GE home show in 1964 is gone. Energy isn't plentiful or cheap anymore. We're humbled by the failure of the nuclear age to live up to its promises. We worry about the still-expanding world population's strain on the planet's resources.

My ideal *post*-postmodern version of the General Electric Progressland would include a new diorama for the early twenty-first century. Instead of symbols of plentiful energy, today's kitchen scene might bear some resemblance to the Great Depression, not in its technology or looks, but in the restraint we'll begin to exercise there. We are on the verge of a time when typical Americans no longer bask in the convenience, but must tally the energy-burning. My new act would include the following dialogue:

> **Father: "Our parents thought that nuclear fusion would create cheap and limitless electricity. Today we know that hasn't come true. We're practicing energy conservation right here at home—Mom got rid of the extra television, the free-standing freezer, and the extra fridge that held the soda and beer."**
> **Mother: "We don't even miss them! What were we thinking?"**

Lighting, cooking, and appliances use 33 percent of the energy in a typical home, according to the U.S. Department of Energy. Many appliances have become greatly efficient, particularly the major workhorses like the refrigerator, clothes washer, and dishwasher. To compare new models of these to their counterparts of a decade ago shows a major savings in energy. But we continue to use more power! The Michigan-based Consumers Energy, one of the largest utility companies in the nation, has found that for the past two decades, the average increase in power use per household has been 1% a year.[2] How could this be? It could be our laziness in failing to turn things off. The most logical reason, I think, is that we live with dozens more appliances than we had in 1964.

Now is the time to turn our attention to the whole second category of appliances—the unnecessary.

One way to figure out which appliances you can discard is to consider the advice of emergency preparedness experts, who often recommend unplugging unnecessary appliances when the forecast is for thunder and lightning. Anything you can do without before a storm deserves closer scrutiny. Many—not all—of the things you'd unplug in a crisis are expendable appliances at other times, also. Some appliances are *always* expendable. Which ones you can ditch depends somewhat on your particular lifestyle and locale. Consider dispensing with the following appliances. Under each, I've estimated the typical amount of energy a household would need and converted it to kilowatt-hours. The financial cost here is not the cost of buying each appliance, but only the cost of the electricity to run it. Clearly, you have to take the initial cost of the appliance into account too.

FREE-STANDING FREEZER, 345 WATTS

Environmental cost: 1,007 kilowatt-hours a year.
Annual financial cost: $85 to $146

Our 345-watt free-standing freezer seemed the perfect money-saving solution. We'd buy bargain food and freeze it. We'd save more money than it cost to run the freezer. Assuming it actually runs for about eight hours out of every twenty-four, the environmental cost of this freezer is 2.76 kilowatt-hours each day, or 1,007 kilowatt hours per year. At our current rate of electricity—14.5 cents per kilowatt-hour—we are paying $146 a year to store food. Even at a typical lower rate found throughout much of America, 8.5 cents per kilowatt-hour, the freezer would still cost $85 a year to run.

Financially, you could justify this. All a shopper has to save is a few dollars a week on food that could be frozen for later use. I used to think that for us, storing food saved not only money but also energy—energy in the form of gas saved by making fewer trips to the store. But this isn't true for us. We live near the center of our town, a half mile from the local supermarket. We live eighteen miles from the discount big-box supermarket where I used to search for most of the frozen bargains. Each trip to that wholesale store now costs several dollars in gas. Then we pay more to store it for months on end. This freezer isn't worth it for us unless I begin shopping much more efficiently for bargains, thereby reducing the number of car trips to the store. With our supermarket so close by, that will take some doing. I have a friend who freezes her garden produce and who diligently stockpiles bargains in the freezer. For her family, the freezer deserves to stay. Look at yours and ask yourself, who needs it more—you, or the environment?

CLOTHES DRYER, 3,400 WATTS

Environmental cost: 1,862 kilowatt-hours a year.
Annual financial cost: $158 to $270

These figures assume the dryer handles ten loads a week, or two loads on each of five days. This means that each load costs just over fifty cents.

I feel guilty criticizing the dryer, which my own mother said so changed her life that she would never go back. She has described

This time-honored way of drying clothes deserves to be revisited.
Image © Index Stock

scenes of chaos with the wet clothes in her Philadelphia back yard in the 1940s. The wooden clothesline props would routinely slip, dragging the wet fabric into the wet grass. Or it would start raining and she, her sisters, and her mother would run outside and scramble to take the clothes in. I don't blame her for loving her dryer. And yet, dryers gobble energy. The viable alternative to dryers—hanging clothes to dry—uses no energy but adds fifteen minutes to your time (per load). In times like these, the dryer must fall under new scrutiny. Someone could invent better clothes-hanging devices than sagging ropes and rickety clothes-props.

MICROWAVE OVEN, 1,000 WATTS

Environmental cost: 183 kilowatt-hours a year.
Annual financial cost: $15.50 to $26.46

At the risk of sounding like a barbarian, I contend that no one need own a microwave oven, even though it uses less energy than most regular ovens. I have assumed that the microwave runs for a half hour a day, all year. Most of what a microwave does well requires no extra source of electricity at all. Microwaves reheat drinks that could stay warm in an insulated jug. Microwaves defrost food that could defrost in the refrigerator over a few hours. Microwaves heat mediocre premade meals. The main problem, though, is that no matter how efficient a microwave may be, it cannot completely replace a regular oven. It can't brown or broil anything, for instance. You will still use your regular oven, perhaps even while you are running the microwave.

If you must own a microwave, at least be honest about its place in the kitchen. It is a convenience, not an energy saver.

GARBAGE DISPOSAL, 800 WATTS

Environmental cost: 21 kilowatt-hours a year.
Annual financial cost: A few dollars

It's not easy to stand up against something that costs so little to operate, but garbage disposals are not necessary in any but the most cramped urban conditions. Out of the city, you can compost the garbage for free.

ELECTRIC BLANKET, 100 WATTS

Environmental cost: 74 kilowatt-hours a year.
Annual financial cost: $6.32 to $10.78

A double-sized 100-watt electric blanket seems harmless. But you might use this for eight hours a night for the three coldest months of the year, consuming 74 kilowatt hours a year. At 8.5 cents a kilowatt hour, that costs $6.32 a year. At my rate of 14.5 cents, it costs $10.78. This is a pure luxury item. The only way you could justify it otherwise is if you had no heat in the house.

HAIR DRYER

Environmental cost: 78 kilowatt-hours a year.
Annual financial cost: $6.63 to $11.31

I admit I don't fuss with my hair. Therefore, I can't see spending fifteen minutes a day holding one of these heated monsters. Hair dryers do the job fast, but the alternative, air drying, uses no electricity at all. The question to ask yourself is: What does a hair dryer provide, and is it worth paying and using energy for this? The benefits might be that a hair dryer saves some embarrassment in public, since you don't have to go out with a wet head.

TRASH COMPACTOR, 1,500 WATTS

Environmental cost: 113 kilowatt-hours a year.
Annual financial cost: $9.56 to $16.31

Here, I assume that the compactor runs for fifteen minutes a day on three hundred days of the year. Compactors, invented in the 1970s, make sense only if space is the issue. Where I live, our trash is incinerated, so there's little point in compacting it. At a large office building or school or factory, using a commercial compactor could save maintenance workers' time emptying trash bins. At home, you'd be better off reducing what you throw in the trash can.

ELECTRIC CAN OPENER, 175 WATTS

Environmental cost: Only the cost of manufacturing it.
Annual financial cost: Pennies

I include the electric can opener as a symbol of the unnecessary. These things make a tremendous amount of noise and take up room in the kitchen. What's the point of owning one, unless for health reasons you can't operate a manual can opener?

One appliance about which I've changed my mind

TOASTER OVEN, 1,100 WATTS, OR TOASTER, 1,200 WATTS

A toaster oven uses a third to a half as much energy as a conventional-size oven. Baking something small in a toaster oven clearly saves energy. A toaster oven also uses about the same amount of power as a regular toaster. If you use either of these to toast bread, the amount of time the appliance runs costs only pennies a day.

Consumers of the world, unite. You have nothing to lose but your utility bill.

Appendix:
Where to Learn More

GENERAL INFORMATION ABOUT ENERGY, CONSUMPTION, AND ALTERNATIVES

U.S. Energy Information Administration, www.eia.doe.gov.

The National Renewable Energy Lab, part of the U.S. Department of Energy, began in the 1970s as the Solar Research Institute. Its main offices in Golden, Colorado, are the headquarters of divisions covering solar energy, wind energy, and biomass. The labs also study energy efficiency, hybrid car technology, geothermal technology, and how to integrate alternative energy into national policies. The NREL Visitors Center is located at 15013 Denver West Parkway, Golden, CO 80401-3393. For information, call 303-384-6565, or go to www.nrel.gov.

American Council for an Energy-Efficient Economy (ACEEE)
1001 Connecticut Avenue, NW, Suite 801
Washington, DC 20036
202-429-8873
or

2140 Shattuck Avenue, Suite 202

Berkeley, CA 94704

ACEEE provides general and technical information on energy effi-ciency, including these publications: *The Consumer Guide to Home En-ergy Savings, The Most Energy-Efficient Appliances*, and *Saving Energy and Money with Home Appliances*. They can be ordered by writing the ACEEE office in Berkeley.

California Energy Commission, www.energy.ca.gov/

To reach its Renewable Energy & Consumer Energy Efficiency In-formation line, call toll-free in California, 1-800-555-7794. Outside California, 916-654-4058.

Good, basic discussions of skills needed to save energy, heat with wood, and insulate the house can be found in: John and Martha Storey, *Storey's Basic Country Skills: A Practical Guide to Self-Reliance* (Pownal, VT: Storey Books, 1991).

PERIODICALS

While many magazines and newspapers report on energy, pollution, and research, these three go beyond the general to explain the tech-nology of alternative energy in clear language.

Home Power

A bimonthly magazine with practical articles for laypeople on using renewable energy at home.

P.O. Box 520

Ashland, OR 97520

For subscription information, go to www.homepower.com/magazine.

Mother Earth News

A bimonthly magazine on self-sufficient living.

Ogden Publications, Inc.

1503 SW 42nd Street

Topeka, KS 66609-1265

To subscribe, call 1-800-234-3369, or go to www.motherearthnews.com.

Wired

A monthly magazine covering all aspects of new technology, including alternative vehicles.

660 Third Street

San Francisco, CA 94107

To subscribe, call 1-800-SOWIRED or 1-303-678-0354, send an e-mail to subscriptions@wiredmag.com, or go to www.wiredmag.com.

CHAPTER 1 – THE SITUATION TODAY

Energy Bulletin

This compendium of information about the world oil supply reprints U.S. Rep. Roscoe Bartlett's presentation on March 14, 2005 at: www.energybulletin.net/4733.htm

American Association for the Study of Peak Oil and Gas

This organization of European scientists can be contacted at

Box 25182, SE-750 25

Uppsala, Sweden

Go to www.peakoil.net

CHAPTER 2 – DEMYSTIFYING SOLAR ENERGY

Finding a Solar Dealer

There are hundreds of solar dealers in the United States and else-where. For the most current list, contact your state government or

Solarbuzz USA

P.O. Box 475815

San Francisco, CA 94147-5815

Call 415-928-9743, or send an e-mail to info@solarbuzz.com, or go to www.solarbuzz.com (click on "Products").

State governments in twenty-three states offer rebate and incentive programs to buy solar panels as of April 2005. For an up-to-date list of programs, contact your state government, or view a detailed list published by the Database of State Incentives for Renewable Energy, www.dsireusa.org.

Gail Burrington provided data and background on appliances and systems.

Burrington's Solar Edge

6 Reed Circle

Windsor Locks, CT 06096

Call 860-623-0159, or go to www.angelfire.com/biz/solaredge.

The Solar Energy Industries Association is a trade organization in Washington, D.C., that speaks for the industry and gives out infor-mation for potential buyers. Contact the association at:

805 15th Street NW

Washington, DC 20005

Call 202-682-0556, or go to www.seia.org.

The Consortium for Advanced Residential Buildings (CARB) is a coalition of house designers and builders and product manufacturers that is working with the U.S. Department of Energy to develop energy-efficient building techniques for new houses. Contact CARB through:

Michael J. Crosbie

Steven Winter Associates, Inc.

50 Washington Street

Norwalk, CT 06854

To read the newsletter go to www.carb-swa.com/carbnews-archive.html.

For information on solar water heaters, see *Selecting a New Water Heater*, a booklet from the Energy Efficiency and Renewable Energy Clearinghouse of the National Renewable Energy Lab. This is helpful, although it was published in 1995.

For information on solar roofing shingles, I can't recommend products, but for more information about shingles that double as solar panels, consult Kyocera Solar, Inc., which makes a residential roof system called MyGen Meridian. For details, go to the Kyocera Web site at www.kyocerasolar.com/products/meridian.html. Or consult United Solar Ovonic of Auburn Hills, Michigan, which makes a kind of solar panel that resembles a roll of plastic. The material is available as shingles, or it can cover metal roofs and awnings. For details, go to http://www.uni-solar.com.

Direct-Current Solar Appliances

Another way to start small is to invest in solar-powered appliances, each attached to individual solar panels that send direct current to the appliance. (No inverter to convert to alternating current is necessary, because these don't connect to the household electrical system.) One of the most logical and useful solar-powered appliances is the solar-powered attic fan, also called an attic vent. It looks like a rectangular solar panel on the roof, but it includes a fan that blows hot air out of the house. The fan receives the most power from the solar unit during the time the house needs the fan the most—on hot, sunny days. These fans typically cost hundreds of dollars. Or try a solar-powered sump pump that won't have to rely on the electricity supply of the house, which might shut down during a flood. Individual solar panels hook up to power laptop computers and other communication devices for field work or travel. Call any solar dealer to ask about these products, or search the Web to learn more. Direct-current solar appliances even turn up on the Web auction site, eBay.

CHAPTER 3 – WIND

The American Wind Energy Association is a trade association based in Washington, D.C. It offers much information about wind power on a small scale and a utility scale, and periodically issues opinions on government policies and reports. Contact the AWEA at:

122 C Street NW, Suite 380

Washington, DC 20001

Call 202-383-2500, or go to www.awea.org.

For California residents, rebates for wind projects are available through the California Energy Commission Buydown Program:

1516 Ninth Street

Sacramento, CA 95814

Call 916-654-4058, or go to www.consumerenergycenter.org/buydown/index.html.

Buying a Small Wind Electric System: A California Consumer's Guide (Sacramento: California Energy Commission, 2002). This can be downloaded from www.energy.ca.gov/renewables/documents/education_documents.html#materials.

For a list of small wind turbines and dealers in California, contact the Consumer Energy Center of the California Energy Commission
    1516 Ninth Street
    Sacramento, CA 95814-5504
Call 916-654-4287, send an e-mail to renewable@energy.state.ca.us, or go to www.consumerenergycenter.org.

The federal government's National Wind Technology Center is located at the National Renewable Energy Center outside Boulder, Colorado. Go to www.nrel.gov/wind.

For general information on choosing a wind generator, see the article by Mick Sagrillo, "Apples and Oranges: Choosing a Home-Sized Wind Generator," *Home Power*, no. 90, August–September 2002, 50.

CHAPTER 4 – HYDROGEN FUEL CELLS AND OTHER NEW ENERGY SOURCES

International Association for Hydrogen Energy, www.iahe.org

Hydrogen Energy Center, www.h2eco.org

International Ground Source Heat Pump Association (IGSHPA) of Stillwater, Oklahoma, www.igshpa.okstate.edu.

Geothermal Heat Pump Consortium, www.geoexchange.org

CHAPTER 5 – HEATING WITH WOOD

To locate retailers of woodstoves and heaters, contact:
Hearth, Patio & Barbecue Association
1601 North Kent Street, Suite 1001
Arlington, VA 22209
Call 703-522-0086, or go to www.hpba.org.

Natural Resources Canada of Ottawa, Ontario, operates a Web site that amounts to **a tutorial on woodstove use**: "Burn It Smart," at www.burnitsmart.org.

The U.S. Department of Energy's National Renewable Energy Laboratory recommends:

Chimney Safety Institute of America. To learn about safely venting a woodstove, see www.csia.org.

Hearth Education Foundation. To learn about installing and using woodstoves, see www.heartheducation.org.

Wood Heat. A Canadian nonprofit organization that teaches responsible use of wood at home. Go to www.woodheat.org.

The Chimney Safety Institute of America
2155 Commercial Drive
Plainfield, IN 46168
Call 317-837-5362, or go to www.csia.org.
The institute provides a national listing of certified chimney sweeps, and information on chimneys and venting combustion appliances.

U.S. Environmental Protection Agency Indoor Air Quality Information Clearinghouse. For publications on indoor air quality, including those concerning wood heating, go to www.epa.gov/iaq/iaqxline.html.

EPA Wood Heater Program. Certifies wood-heating appliances and provides information on wood heating. Go to www.epa.gov/compliance and click on Wood Heater Program.

Hearth Education Foundation. A nonprofit organization to teach the public and professionals about installing and using wood-burning appliances. Go to www.heartheducation.org.

Masonry Heater Association of North America
1252 Stock Farm Road
Randolph, VT 05060
Call 802-728-5896, or go to www.mha-net.org.

CHAPTER 6 – HARNESSING A BACKYARD STREAM: MICRO-HYDROELECTRIC SYSTEMS

National Hydropower Association, www.hydro.org.

Idaho National Engineering and Environmental Laboratory
http://hydropower.id.doe.gov/resourceassessment/states.shtml.

United States Society on Dams
1616 Seventeenth Street, #483
Denver, Colorado 80202
Call 303-628-5430, fax 303-628-5431, or send an e-mail to stephens @ussdams.org.

CHAPTER 7 – ALTERNATIVE CARS

Edmunds.com is a Web-based magazine that independently rates cars and trucks, www.edmunds.com.

Stacy C. Davis and Susan W. Diegel, *Transportation Energy Data Book*, *Edition 24*. (Knoxville, TN: Oak Ridge National Laboratory, 2004), http://cta.ornl.gov/data/index.shtml.

CHAPTER 8 – CONSERVATION

Energy Efficiency and Renewable Energy Program of the U.S. Department of Energy. For numerous fact sheets about alternative energy on the Web, go to www.eere.energy.gov/consumerinfo/factsheets.html.

See also **Energy Savers: Tips on Saving Money and Energy at Home** at www.eere.energy.gov/energy_savers/order.html

Alex Wilson, Jennifer Thorne, and John Morrill, **Consumer Guide to Home Energy Savings** (Washington, DC: American Council for an Energy-Efficient Economy, 2003).

Natural Resources Defense Council. This New York-based advocacy and lobbying organization produces consumer guides to energy conservation. Call 212-727-2700, or go to www.nrdc.org.

CHAPTER 9 – CONSERVATION TIPS

For general information:

U.S. Department of Energy's Energy Efficiency and Renewable Energy Clearinghouse

Call 800-DOE-3732, or go to www.eere.energy.gov/buildings/homes/insulatinghome.cfm.

Energy Savers: Tips on Saving Energy & Money at Home
A thirty-six-page booklet produced by the U.S. Department of Energy, Energy Efficiency and Renewable Energy Department

1000 Independence Avenue SW

Washington, DC 20585.

Go to www.eere.energy.gov/consumer/.

Under the federal Energy Policy Act of 2005, people may deduct some of their costs for energy-efficiency improvements on their tax returns as follows:

- Consumers can receive a credit of up to 30% of the cost, or up to $2,000, for installing solar-powered hot-water systems used exclusively for purposes other than heating swimming pools and hot tubs.

- Consumers can receive tax credits of up to $500 on the amount they spend to upgrade thermostats, to caulk leaks, or to stop energy waste.

- Consumers can receive up to $200 credit for installation of new exterior windows.

- Consumers can receive up to $300 credit for purchases of a highly efficient central air conditioner, heat pump, or water heater.

- Consumers can receive up to $150 for installation of a highly efficient furnace or boiler.

- A new provision provides a 10% investment tax credit for expenditures with respect to improvements to building envelope.

- Allows credits for purchases of advanced main air circulating fans, natural gas, propane, or oil furnaces or hot water boilers, and other qualified energy-efficient property.

- Tax credits for contractors who build energy-efficient homes and manufacturers who make energy-efficient appliances could lower prices for consumers.

SOURCE: the U.S. Department of Energy

No-Electricity Gadgets

Manual coffee grinder. Reasonably priced at the Vermont Country Store. Call 1-802-362-8460, or go to http://vermontcountrystore.com.

Wind-up Radios and Flashlights. Innovative Technologies sells hand-powered necessities invented by Trevor Baylis. Call 1-888-322-1455, or go to www.windupradio.com.

Solar Shower Bags. Camping and boating devices allow you to hang a bag of water in the sun. When heated, you stand beneath it and open the valve. It's a short shower, but effective. For one model, see the Raytech catalog at www.raytechcatalog.com.

CHAPTER 10 – AN APPLIANCE MANIFESTO

The federal Energy Information Administration compiles reports on people's use of electricity and appliances at home. The administration is a program of the U.S. Department of Energy in Washington, D.C. To read the reports, press releases, and other data, go to www.eia.doe.gov.

Notes

To ensure that readers may easily locate Web-based articles that may have been moved around a site, for some of the links, I have listed the home page, from which the article can be found by searching.

INTRODUCTION

1. Paul Maidment, "The High Price of Oil," *Forbes*, August 9, 2004, www.forbes.com/energy/2004/08/09/cx_pm_0611oilbrief.html.
2. Oregon State University, Department of Political Science, "Gasoline Prices in Current and Constant Cents Per Gallon, 1950 to 2004," a chart based upon data from the United States Energy Information Administration, www.oregonstate.edu/Dept/pol_sci/fac/sahr/gasol.htm.

CHAPTER 1 – THE SITUATION TODAY

1. United States Energy Information Administration, www.eia.gov. Information also available on the Conoco Phillips Web site, www.conocophillips.com/newsroom/other_resources/energyanswers/future_supply.htm.

2. David Deming, "Are We Running Out of Oil?" a "Policy Back-grounder" article of the National Center for Policy Analysis, www.ncpa.org/pub/bg/bg159/index.html#c. Deming writes, "By the year 2000, a total of 900 billion barrels of oil had been produced. Total world oil production in 2000 was 25 billion barrels. If world oil consumption continues to increase at an average rate of 1.4% a year, and no further resources are discovered, the world's oil supply will not be exhausted until the year 2056."

3. President George W. Bush, "President Discusses Energy Policy" (speech, Ronald Reagan Building and International Trade Center Washington, D.C., June 15, 2005) www.whitehouse.gov.

4. James A. Fay and Dan S. Golumb, *Energy and the Environment* (New York: Oxford University Press, 2002), 23.

5. U.S. Energy Information Administration of the U.S. Department of Energy, www.eia.doe.gov. This refers to data showing that 40% of America's energy sources come from petroleum.

6. Web site of the Society of Petroleum Engineers of Richardson, Texas, www.spe.org.

7. PFC Energy, "PFC Energy's Global Crude Oil and Natural Gas Liquids Supply Forecast" (PowerPoint presentation, Washington, D.C., September 2004); cited in Stark, Linda, editor, Worldwatch Institute, *Vital Signs 2005* (New York: Norton, 2005), 30.

8. Energy experts, writers, and the U.S. Department of Energy all have described the Peak Oil concept. U.S. Rep. Roscoe Bartlett of Maryland went into detail about it in a presentation he gave in March 2005 to the U.S. House of Representatives.

9. Fay and Golumb, *Energy and the Environment,* 25. Concise description of the oil shale reserves.

10. Energy briefing on the United States, Web site of the U.S. Department of Energy, Energy Information Administration, www.eia.doe.gov/emeu/cabs/usa.html.

11. Fay and Golumb, *Energy and the Environment,* 23.

12. Bruce Murray, "Assessing the East Coast Blackout: Was Deregulation to Blame?" Facsnet.com, August 19, 2003, www.facsnet.org/tools/energy/blackout.php. Severin Borenstein, professor of business administration and public policy at the University of California, Berkeley, is quoted in this article. Also, Associated Press wire service, "How the Power Grid System Works," August 14, 2003.

13. U.S.-Canada Power System Outage Task Force, "Final Report on the August 14, 2003, Blackout in the United States and Canada: Causes and Recommendations." April 2004, available online from the Harvard Electricity Policy Group, www.ksg.harvard.edu.

14. "Interview with James Kunstler," *High Country News,* June 13, 2005, 13. See also Kunstler's books, *The Long Emergency: Surviving the Converging Catastrophes of the Twenty-first Century* (New York: Atlantic Monthly Press, 2005), and earlier titles, *Geography of Nowhere: The Rise and Decline of America's Man-Made Landscape* (New York: Touchstone, 1994), and *Home From Nowhere: Remaking Our Everyday World* (New York: Touchstone, 1996).

15. Fay and Golumb, *Energy and the Environment,* 27.

CHAPTER 2 – DEMYSTIFYING SOLAR ENERGY

1. Jimmy Carter, "The President's Proposed Energy Policy," (televised speech, April 18, 1977), *Vital Speeches of the Day,* 43,

no. 14 (May 1, 1977), 418–20. Available online at
www.pbs.org/wgbh/amex/carter/filmmore/ps_energy.html.

2. Telephone interviews by author with Peter Marbach, former
development director at Unity College, and other staffers at
Unity College, solar installers, and others, 1997 through 2005.

3. Most of these facts come from the *CIA World Factbook,* a com-
pilation of government statistics (see www.cia.gov). My
source here is Nationmaster.com, a Web site that compiles
statistics on many countries.

4. Mark Gielecki, Fred Mayes, and Lawrence Prete, "Incentives,
Mandates, and Government Programs for Promoting Renewable
Energy," U.S. Energy Information Administration of the U.S.
Department of Energy, www.eia.doe.gov/cneaf/solar.renew-
ables/rea_issues/incent.html. The federal government offered
homeowners tax credits of 30% of the first $2,000 and 20% of
the next $8,000 for solar and wind equipment. In 1980, the
incentives increased to 30% to 40% of the first $10,000 and
added geothermal technology to the equipment covered. By
1985, the government had stopped offering the credits.

5. Janet L. Sawin, "Solar Energy Markets Booming," *Vital Signs
2005*, 36.

6. Sawin, "Solar Energy Markets Booming," *Vital Signs 2005,* 36.

7. Interview by the author with homeowner and solar dealer Ed
Witkin of Bridgewater, Connecticut, March 2005.

8. Telephone interview by the author with Gail Burrington,
owner of Burrington's Solar Edge, Windsor, Connecticut,
March 2005.

9. *Connecticut Consumer's Guide to Buying a Solar Electric System*
(Rocky Hill: Connecticut Clean Energy Fund), 3. This is based
on a guide by Tom Starrs and Howard Wenger for the Califor-

nia Energy Commission with the National Renewable Energy Laboratory, Golden, Colorado.

10. Michael J. Crosbie, "Cutting the Power," *CARB News* (Vol. 8, No. 9, March 2005) the newsletter of the Consortium for Advanced Residential Buildings, a project of the Building America Program sponsored partly by the U.S. Department of Energy. *CARB News* is published by Steven Winter Associates of Norwalk, Connecticut, www.carb-swa.com/carbnews-archive.html.

11. Interview by the author with homeowner Peter Markow, Tolland, Connecticut, April 2005.

CHAPTER 3 – WIND GENERATORS AT HOME

1. Michael T. Eckhart, "Renewable Energy 2005: A Mid-Year Review," www.renewableenergyaccess.com. RenewableEnergy Access.com is a Web publication covering the alternative energy industry. Michael Eckhart is president of the American Council on Renewable Energy.

2. Calvin R. Trice, "Residents in Highland Vent about Wind Farm," *Richmond Times-Dispatch,* May 21, 2005.

3. "An Assessment of the Available Windy Land Area and Wind Energy Potential in the Contiguous United States," Pacific Northwest Laboratory, 1991. Available from American Wind Energy Association, www.awea.org.

4. Fay and Golumb, *Energy and the Environment,* 166–67.

5. Interview by the author with Mick Sagrillo. Measurements include examples of wind systems found advertised for sale in 2005.

6. Steve Raabe, "Elbert Couple Cuts Energy Bills with Small Wind Turbine," *Denver Post,* May 18, 2005.

CHAPTER 4 – OTHER NEW TECHNOLOGIES

1. *The Hydrogen Economy: Opportunities, Costs, Barriers, and R&D Needs* (Washington, DC: National Academies Press, 2004), 45. (www.nap.edu/books)

2. Energy Independence Now, Santa Monica, California, fact sheet on hydrogen fuel cells, "What Is A Fuel Cell and How Does It Work?" See also www.fuelcells.org.

3. Fay and Golumb, *Energy and the Environment,* 65.

4. Hydrogenics Corporation of Mississauga, Ontario, "Hydrogenics Signs Contract to Provide Fuel Cell System for U.S. Army Armoured Vehicle," May 25, 2005. Hydrogenics is a fuel-cell developer.

5. Kettering University, Flint, Michigan, "Partnership Will Put Fuel-Cell Bus on Flint Streets," May 9, 2005.

6. Seth Dunn, "Hydrogen Futures: Toward a Sustainable Energy System," Worldwatch Institute Paper 157 (Washington, DC: Worldwatch Institute, August 2001).

7. Natural Resources Defense Council, www.nrdc.org.

8. World Fuel Cell Council, www.fuelcellworld.org, is based in Germany.

9. Dunn, "Hydrogen Futures," 7–8.

10. Kunstler, *The Long Emergency*, as excerpted in *Rolling Stone,* March 2005.

11. World Fuel Cell Council, www.fuelcellworld.org.

12. Jim Motavalli, "Putting the Hindenburg to Rest," *The New York Times,* June 5, 2005, sec. 12, p. 1.

13. Alternative Fuels Data Center of the U.S. Department of Energy's Energy Efficiency and Renewable Energy program, www.eere.energy.gov.

14. "Heat Your Home with Biodiesel," *Mother Earth News*, no. 201, December–January, 2004.

15. Interview by the author with Nevin Christensen, May 2005.

16. Throughout this section, I have relied heavily on information from the California Energy Commission in Sacramento, which offers a wealth of information and facts through its Web site, known as the Consumer Energy Center, www.consumerenergy center.org.

CHAPTER 5 – HEATING WITH WOOD

1. United States Environmental Protection Agency, Technology Transfer Network Air Toxics Web site, www.epa.gov/ttn/atw/hlthef/polycycl.html.

2. Lawrence H. Fisher, James E. Houck, Paul E. Tiegs, and James McGaughey, *Long-Term Performance of EPA-Certified Phase 2 Woodstoves: Klamath Falls and Portland, Oregon.* (Cincinnati, Ohio: National Risk Management Research Laboratory, 1998–1999).

3. U.S. Department of Energy, Office of Energy Efficiency and Renewable Energy, online consumer fact sheet on heating with wood, www.eere.energy.gov.

4. Maine's Department of Environmental Protection, explaining EPA regulations, www.maine.gov/dep/air/education/woodstv.htm.

5. Summarizing the argument neatly is consumer advocate Debra Lynn Dadd in "Why Wood Is the Best Fuel, "www.worldwise .com/whywoodisbes.html.

6. University of New Hampshire Climate Education Initiative, *UNH Greenhouse Gas Emissions Inventory 1990–2003* (Durham:

University of New Hampshire, July 2004). UNH cites the U.S. Environmental Protection Agency.

7. Telephone interview by the author with Dirk Thomas of Cuttingsville, Vermont. Thomas is the author of *The Wood Burner's Companion* (Chambersburg, PA: Allen C. Hood, 2004). Also, from a telephone interview by the author with Bartok, April 2005.

8. "The End of the Wood Stove? An Interview with Dan Melcon, Industry Gadfly and Fellow Alarmist," *Mother Earth News,* Issue 170, October–November 1998.

9. "Home Heating with Wood," Clemson University Cooperative Extension Service, May 1988.

10. John and Martha Storey, *Storey's Basic Country Skills* (Pownal, VT: Storey Publishing, 1999), 61.

11. Don Hopey, "Wood Treatment Linked to Dangers," *Pittsburgh Post-Gazette,* January 25, 1998.

12. Telephone interview by the author with John Bartok, of Ashford, Connecticut, a retired agricultural engineer with the University of Connecticut, April 2005.

CHAPTER 6: HARNESSING A BACKYARD STREAM: MICRO-HYDROELECTRIC SYSTEMS

1. U.S. Department of Energy, Office of Energy Efficiency and Renewable Energy, information about the hydroelectric program of the U.S. Department of Energy, Wind and Water Technologies Program, http://www.eere.energy.gov/windandhydro/.

2. For background about dams and hydroelectric plants, I consulted E. C. Pielou, *Fresh Water* (Chicago: University of Chicago

Press, 1998). Information about the Hoover Dam is from the U.S. Bureau of Reclamation, http://www.usbr.gov/lc/hoover dam/faqs/powerfaq.html. Information about the Grand Coulee Dam is from http://users.owt.com/chubbard/gcdam.

3. Paul Cunningham and Barbara Atkinson,"Micro Hydro Power in the 1990s," *Home Power,* no. 44, December 1994–January 1995, 24–29; Juliette and Lucien Gunderman, "Powerful Dreams: Crown Hill Farm's Hydro Electric Plant," *Home Power,* no. 96, August–September 2003, 14–21; Dan New, "Intro to Hydro Power," *Home Power,* no. 103, October–November 2004, 14–20.

CHAPTER 7: ALTERNATIVE CARS

1. Stacy C. Davis and Susan W. Diegel, *Transportation Energy Data Book: Edition 24* (Oak Ridge, TN: Oak Ridge National Laboratory, 2004).
2. Telephone interview by the author with Jeff Deyette, Union of Concerned Scientists in Boston, June 2005.
3. Connecticut General Assembly, Special Act No. 05-06, "An Act Concerning a Connecticut Clean Car Incentive Program," June 24, 2005.
4. Jim Motavalli, "What a Gas! A Week in Suburbia with a Hydrogen Honda," *The New York Times,* June 5, 2005, sec. 12, p. 1.
5. "How a Hybrid Works," Edmunds.com, the Web car magazine. See www.edmunds.com.
6. Mario F. Teisl, Jonathan Rubin, Caroline Noblet, Lynn Cayting, Melissa Morrill, Thomas Brown, and Sue Jones, *Designing Effective Environmental Labels for Passenger Vehicles in Maine:*

Results of Focus Group Research, Miscellaneous Report 434 (Orono: University of Maine, Maine Agricultural and Forest Experiment Station, December 2004).
7. Gas mileage and efficiency rankings for regular and hybrid cars are from www.edmunds.com.

CHAPTER 8: CONSERVATION

1. James Brooke, "Is a Salaryman without a Suit Like Sushi without the Rice?" *The New York Times,* Friday, May 20, 2005, A1, C4.
2. Allen Best, "How Dense Can We Be," *High Country News,* June 13, 2005, 10–11.
3. Best, "How Dense Can We Be," 11.
4. Christine Woodside, "Oasis on the Edge," *The Hartford Courant,* September 7, 2003, C4.
5. U.S. Department of Energy, Office of Energy Efficiency and Renewable Energy, *Energy Savers,* www.eere.energy.gov/consumer/tips/.
6. Kenneth T. Jackson, "Public Transportation: The Twentieth Century," *Reader's Companion to American History,* http://college.hmco.com/history/readerscomp/rcah/html/ah _072007_thetwentieth.htm.
7. Lindsey Grant, *The Collapsing Bubble: Growth and Fossil Energy* (Santa Ana, CA: Seven Locks Press, 2005), 5.
8. "Low Cost, Abundant Energy: Paradise Lost?" *Science,* 184, no. 4134 (April 19, 1974). I cite the version anthologized in *Readings on Energy Conservation: Selected Materials compiled by the Congressional Research Service at the Request of Henry M. Jackson, Chairman, Committee on Interior and Insular*

Affairs, United States Senate (Washington, DC: U.S. Government Printing Office, 1975).

9. Gary Althen, *American Ways: A Guide for Foreigners in the United States* (Yarmouth, Maine: Intercultural Press, 2002).

10. Telephone interview by the author with Paul Cunningham, June 2005.

11. Elliot Aronson and Michael O'Leary, "The Relative Effectiveness of Models and Prompts on Energy Conservation: A Field Experiment in a Shower Room." *Journal of Environmental Systems*, 12, 219–224. This study is cited in numerous research papers.

12. Chauncey Starr, "Realities of the Energy Crisis," in *Perspectives on Energy: Issues, Ideas, and Environmental Dilemmas*, ed. Lon C. Ruedisili and Morris W. Firebaugh (New York: Oxford University Press, 1975).

CHAPTER 10: AN APPLIANCE MANIFESTO

1. For Walt Disney's impact on how we view modern appliances, valuing convenience in appliances, go to http://www.yesterland.com/progress.html.

2. Interview by the author with Jeff Holyfield, director of news and information, Consumers Energy, Jackson, Michigan.

3. To calculate the electricity appliances use, I followed the instructions of the U.S. Department of Energy, Office of Energy Efficiency and Renewable Energy. See www.eere.energy.gov/consumer/your_home/appliances/index.cfm/mytopic=10040. Check the list of common appliances for the range of watts each one puts out. Or, to be more accurate, check the labels or manuals of your appliances. Multiply wattage by the

number of hours the appliance runs each day. Divide this number by 1,000 to calculate the daily kilowatt-hour use, as 1,000 watts equals 1 kilowatt. Finally, multiply this by the number of days you use the appliance each year. You then can calculate your yearly cost to own this appliance by multiplying the kilowatt-hours-per-year figure by your local electricity rate per kilowatt-hour.

Index